The Word of God and Modern Man

The
Word
of God
and Modern
Man

EMIL BRUNNER

Translated by David Cairns

JOHN KNOX PRESS

RICHMOND, VIRGINIA

The original German edition of *Das Wort Gottes und der moderne Mensch* was published and copyrighted by Zwingli-Verlag, Zürich, 1947.

Library of Congress Catalog Card Number: 64-16280

© M. E. Bratcher 1964

Printed in the United States of America

9905(20)6656

CONTENTS

I. THE WORD OF GOD AND MODERN MAN

There is something provocative in the theme "The Word of God and Modern Man," and in the inner tension which it suggests. My first temptation accordingly is to disclaim the responsibility for its formulation and to leave it with those who suggested the theme to me. What has modern man to do with the Word of God, and what has the Word of God to do with modern man?

And yet the theme is there, not through human caprice but through inner necessity. It was not given to me alone; it is given to us all, we cannot evade it. Indeed, it seems at first, at least from one side, as if there were absolutely no connection at all. Modern man—however we may provisionally define him—will above all assert that he is completely uninterested in this other entity, called "The Word of God." We are no longer living in the eighteenth century, when reason first gained self-confidence and still had to struggle violently for mastery with this opponent; neither the struggle against the authority of the Bible nor the struggle against the teaching authority of the Church is a matter which claims the attention of modern man. This phase of the struggle has long ago passed; indeed, the phase which immediately followed it has concluded, the phase of protested indifference. We have entered upon a new phase, the phase of complete incomprehension and irrelevance. People are no longer able to understand how we can even ask a question of this nature. Typical modern man finds even the theme "The Word of God" as a subject for contemporary discussion something quite impossible, almost absurdly antiquated. How can

educated modern man have any concern with such a question?
After all, we live in the present, and not in a museum!

And yet this modern man must acquaint himself with the
fact that there are still a considerable—and growing—number of
men of his own kind and culture who affirm that the Word of
God is the decisive reality in their lives. If the two groups are
not simply to live in isolation from each other—which it is impossible to do permanently, since they are economically and
politically interdependent—the discussion between them must get
under way, even though at first it may seem completely without
prospects of success. The method is indicated precisely by the
provisional lack of contact; there is nothing else left to do except
that each side should state its case and the other should listen.
The case of the one side, that of modern man, can be summed
up very briefly: "I haven't the faintest idea what you on the
other side mean by what you call 'The Word of God.' The claim
that something like a God exists who speaks, or has spoken, or
will speak, seems to me quite absurd, not to say childish. This
thought, which doubtless has played a great part in human history, belongs to a phase of the evolution of human history which
lies far behind us—the age of myth, of the anthropomorphic
picture of the world. Just as primitive men and children per-
sonify everything that encounters them in the outer world, and
treat it as a subject that speaks to them and is to be spoken
to, so mankind in the age of its childhood personified the world
as a whole, and projected upon it the image of a personal,
speaking God, and spoke with him in full conviction of the
reality of the conversation. But since science and the general
development of culture have brought us out of this mythical
phase, more and more these personalistic conceptions of God
have lost their vitality; they have become more and more abstract, and have finally evaporated—for one man into nothing,
for another into the inconceivable mystery of the universe, for
a third into a divine universe—or whatever one may call it."
Modern man, so continues this confession, is perhaps not simply
irreligious, he even acknowledges indeed a holy mystery which
invisibly underlies the visible world, which in Goethe's words

he "honors in silence"; but whether he is a believer or an unbeliever, what distinguishes him absolutely from a believer in the old childlike sense of the word, is this: he has done with every kind of personal conception of God such as finds expression in the concept of "The Word of God." The personal, speaking God—this is mythology, which is incompatible with modern scientific and philosophical culture.

A second argument is perhaps added to this, which has more to do with the concept of value than with that of truth. It is good, we are told, that we modern men have lost this concept of God. It is incompatible with our will to live; it makes man a fugitive from the world, a seeker of the other world, and therefore useless for life. We think of the war waged by one of the creators of the modern spirit, Friedrich Nietzsche, not only against Christianity but against all this "otherworldliness" as he called it, in the name of life, of human power, greatness, and dignity. Everything that in any way comes under the name of faith in God must make us otherworldly, and thus alienate us from this world, from real life. A more recent protagonist of the modern spirit, Nikolai Hartmann, developed Nietzsche's thought to the conclusion: in the name of human freedom we must deny the concept of God; the will to freedom postulates atheism.

There is, in fact, no difficulty in finding examples in the history of the religions, and even in that of Christianity, showing how religion, and particularly the faith in a personal God, hampers life and destroys freedom. To sum up the case put by modern man: "Your thought of a speaking, and thus highly personal, God is mythology incompatible with disciplined thought; but even if it were still thinkable, it would be unwelcome, as a hindrance to life."

1. The Question: What Is Man?

If I am now to pass on to formulate the case of those who claim that the Word of God is the decisive reality in their life (I must from the start exclude all mediating positions), I must first specify two things that I shall not do. In the first place, I shall not use apologetics; that is, I shall not try to refute the arguments of the moderns and thus, so to speak, prove the Christian faith in the Word of God. That might in itself be a meaningful and profitable undertaking—or it might not; at any rate, I shall not embark upon it. And second, it is not my purpose to develop a theological doctrine of the Word of God, taking no account of the fact that we are involved in a conversation with modern men who have no understanding of it. There is plenty of theological doctrine about the Word of God in itself: doctrine which can and must be explicated by reflection purely within the context of faith, and which has been developed from the classical ages of Christian theology and by true masters of the subject. The theologians among us know this, and they know also that my reference to these old masters is no empty phrase. I have, I may say, daily recourse to the teaching of these men, and I can wish nothing better for theologians than that they should do so too. To learn what Augustine, what Anselm of Canterbury, what Luther and Calvin have thought and written upon this theme is still a superb schooling for us today, a schooling of which we can never have enough.

But here we are considering the conversation between us, who are believers, and the others who not only are unbelievers but who simply cannot understand how belief today can possibly hold up its head. And now that I have let the other side find expression—at least briefly, and, I hope, to some purpose— I propose to continue this conversation by trying to show how modern man appears from the standpoint of the Word of God. Then later, in a second part, I shall direct our attention to the light in which we have examined ourselves.

I say "ourselves." For let us not deceive ourselves: all of us are in some way modern men, and the whole skepticism of modern mankind has in some way infected all of us, though in some it is perhaps powerfully held in check by faith, yet in such a manner that the "old man," even if powerless and ineffectual, is still present. But in many—and there are far more of them than would themselves admit it—this modern thought is present as a powerful doubt which with greater or less success menaces their faith and threatens to subvert it. And in the last place, among all those who confess their faith in the Word of God to be the decisive reality in their lives, there is not one who, in coming to believe, did not in some way have modern thought as his background and point of departure. So I am speaking of ourselves when I speak of modern man, and I am speaking of the Word of God when I speak of him. For—and this is my thesis—what modern man really is can only be understood from the standpoint of the Word of God, and, conversely, we can only understand what is meant by the Word of God when we understand what modern man is. Thus it is by no chance that these two things have come together in our title, seeing it is by such a bond of necessity that they are held together.

Modern man is first and foremost man. And the riddle which modern man sets us is first and foremost the riddle of man. The modernity of man—that is, the thing that distinguishes modern man from the man of any other time or cultural epoch—is basically simply a definite understanding of man, a self-understanding. It is about the understanding of man, of ourselves, that primarily the battle is joined between, let us say, Jesus Christ and Friedrich Nietzsche, or between Karl Marx and Christ, or between Sigmund Freud or Max Scheler or Oswald Spengler—or anyone else whom one may choose as the representative of the modern self-understanding—and Christ. For whatever we may think about man, we can never escape this fact,

that he is the thinking being; that whatever else he thinks, he
is in the last resort determined by what he thinks about himself. The life of man—whether it is his science, his technology,
his politics, his economics, his intellectual culture—is always an
exposition, an interpretation of himself which he offers. The
skyscraper just as much as the Gothic cathedral, the capitalist
or communist economic system just as much as Dante's *Divina
Commedia* or Goethe's *Faust*, the democratic constitution of my
native land just as much as the modern dictator states—whatever
else they may be—are, above all, expositions of the self-understanding of man.

2. *Creatureliness*

The Christian faith, which is faith in the Word of God,
understands man as God's creation, as creature. By this, two
opposite possibilities are excluded. *First*, man is not God; he is
in no sense a god. This delimitation seems to be less necessary
in rationalistic Europe than in mystical India, whose ancient
holy teaching culminates in the affirmation that in the last resort
God and man are one, because the innermost in man—his mind,
the thinking part of him—is identical with the primordial thinker,
with Divinity. Modern man is more inclined to regard himself
as a nonentity or as an animal than as a god, and yet the
delimitation on this side is important enough among us too, for
European rationalism itself is merely a modification of the concept of identity, according to which human reason identifies
itself with absolute truth. We shall in a moment follow this
thought in more detail. But first we must turn to the *second*
point. That man is a creature, God's creation, is a delimitation
which warns us not to treat humanity as something profane
or nugatory. True, man is not God, he is neither the first nor
the last; he is not the center and measure of all things; he is
not his own lord and not his own creator: he is a dependent,

subordinate, limited creature. He is—as the Bible says—dust of
the dust.

But the Bible adds to this an important second qualification:
he is created in the image of God. The Christian understanding
of man depends on the understanding of this concept. What
does it mean? Obviously again this: in his nature and being,
man is not independent; the image—we think with the Apostle
Paul of the image in a mirror—receives its content from its
counterpart, whose likeness it is. Man's being is a likeness and
not an original. And that means further, he is a being that re-
flects and gives back, he is not an original giver. Man gives
back what he first receives: his very nature is to receive, and
in receiving to give back and to pass on what he has received.
When we understand this mysterious expression of the Old
Testament, the "image of God," in the light of the New Testament and of Jesus Christ, we are compelled to say, "Man as
created in the image of God is the creature that receives his
particular being in the divine call of love; but he receives it
in such a manner that he only becomes 'himself' by responding
to this call of love with an answering love."

This is the true meaning of the term *imago Dei*, the being
that answers God's Word, the being that must answer to Love
with love. In contrast with things, plants, and animals, man is
the responsible being. While all other created beings are created
with their complete nature stamped upon them, man always
becomes himself only as he takes, as we say, his life in his own
hand, understands himself in a certain way, and makes a certain
decision, and resolution. And indeed—as the Bible tells us—in
this decision of his he is not free, he cannot make it as he
will, but the freedom of his self-determination is from the outset
limited by his God-given destiny. Man is created in order to
determine himself in a determinate manner, that is, in a manner
that answers to the divine summons in love as an answer in
love. The freedom of man is thus not unconditional but conditioned, and not conditioned from without but from within,
not by compulsion but by a summons, so that its converse side,
as freedom, is responsibility.

There is doubtless a great deal more to be said about man: about the human body, its chemical composition and its physiological functioning; about the mechanism of the psychical life; and about the special laws and norms of the mind. All this has its place in the Christian view of man. But just as in the case of a work of art we do not so much inquire about its material presuppositions as about the artistic idea which it expresses, so it is with man. We understand the whole man, even his physical nature, best when we start from this highest point, his true responsibility, while we inevitably misunderstand this highest point if we start from below. Looking at the whole of man, we say man is the responsible being.

There is indeed also a conception of responsibility which does not start so high. But when we look more closely, it then becomes apparent that what is being spoken of is responsibility only in an inauthentic and diluted sense. To take responsibility seriously means to understand man in relation to the call of God, to the Word of God. Only thus do we seriously understand even the meaning or content of responsibility—namely, as the responsibility to love. I do not say that this responsibility can be demonstrated—thank God it cannot be demonstrated! But what can certainly be demonstrated is that only when man is understood in relation to the love of God is it also understood that love is the meaning of responsibility, and that only where man is thus understood in relation to God's call of love is man really understood as responsible.

Thus the Word of God is not a supplementary addition to man's being, something which one man has and another not— just as one man may be a sportsman or a musician and another not. The Word of God is the presupposition of humanity. Man is man in the Word of God. It is precisely this which is meant by the image of God. So, just as God is love, man on his part is created himself to be one who loves, receiving and living in this love of God. This is what the Bible calls faith. And it is for him to give back to the Creator as gratitude the love which he receives. "Let us love him, for he first loved us." And since the Creator cannot himself receive this love of man, since as the source of love God is not in need of love, he gives to man, as the true recipient of this love, his fellow man and his fellow creature. The twofold word "Thou shalt love the Lord thy God with all thy heart and thy neighbor as thyself" does not express a command which in a more or less accidental manner attaches something to humanity. It expresses the original divinely created being of man. This is man as God intends him to be; this is his destiny, and with this destiny his life as a human life is bestowed upon him.

3. The Real Man

Is this *modern* man, or indeed in any sense a *real* man, that we have described here?

The question cannot be answered with a simple "Yes" or "No." We are more tempted to say "No," and there are good grounds for this, but the "Yes" is not simply canceled by this "No." Is not even modern man responsible? Is not even man as he is—in all his wretchedness or hatefulness and enmity to God—destined for love? Whatever else he may be, is not even he God's creature, created in God's image, and for that reason owing love to God and his neighbor? Responsibility does not in fact cease when men run away from it; our destiny, for which we are created, does not cease to be our destiny when we miss the mark in our answer.

On the other hand, it is unquestionable that we are not this being, neither we ourselves nor any one of those whom we know—this being that answers the loving Creator's Word with the loving response of his life, loving his neighbor and living in this love as a truly human man. Reality shows us something different; it shows us that we live in contradiction to this destiny, that we act contrary to this responsibility.

Not everybody feels or experiences this contrast equally

strongly or deeply, but there is no one who is quite unaware
of it; and similarly there is no one who of himself perceives
it *aright*. There is no one who is absolutely unaware of it. Every
man, even the most modern, knows what lovelessness is and,
when he is treated without love, feels that this is something
that ought not to be. In this the consciousness of responsibility
declares itself, no matter what other theory of man may be pro-
fessed. People recognize and acknowledge responsibility; they
have a very lively and sensitive perception of it—if not in their
own case, at least in that of other people. People realize that
others owe us something, and will continue to do so. In this
form the consciousness of responsibility is universal. But what
is the real cause, the deeper reason for lovelessness and irrespon-
sibility, this people of themselves do not know. Only the Word
of God tells us this.

But because we are no longer speaking of man in his original
nature, but of man in his opposition to his origin, this Word of
God has become different. By his revolt against his divinely
ordained destiny, man is not only perverted in his nature and
become self-contradictory—his divine destiny contradicts his own
self-determination—but through this perversion he is no longer
capable of hearing God's Word, of hearing it in its original
form. So long as he retains his human nature, man does indeed
hear something of God's Word; the moment that he ceased to
hear anything of it, he would cease to be a man. But he hears
of it in a way that is determined by his perversion. The Bible
calls this the law written in the heart. The divine Word of
God has changed into the law "Thou shalt." Responsibility, as
we said, is still there, and so is a certain knowledge of responsibility. Man never quite loses this so long as he is a man, although more and more of it is lost to him the further he turns
away from his divine destiny. But this still-present knowledge
of his responsibility has no longer the original content. The
divine call of love has turned into the moral law. Man still
feels that the moral law really means the love of our neighbor,
but this is no longer clear, because the origin, our life in the
love of God, is no longer perceived. For here knowledge and

being are one. Man can only *know* his life in the love of God when he lives in God's love. But because of his turning away from the divine love, through his own perverse choice, he lives no longer in the divine love but *contrary* to it. And therefore he no longer knows the divine love, he knows God in some manner as a hostile power. God becomes an idol to him.

This whole perversion of man's nature by his setting of his own will against his divine destiny, is what the Bible calls sin. It tells us that we are sinners, and means just this, that our life does not stand in the love of God but in contradiction to it. This sin has thus a threefold nature: first, it is a perverted relation to the Creator; second, it is a perversion of our own nature; and third, it is a perversion of our relation to our fellow creature, our fellow man. The perversion of the relation to the Creator is the center. From this all else flows, because man as image of God is always identical with his relation to God. That his relation is a perverted one means expressly that a relation is there. Even in his uttermost godlessness, man is not without a relation to God. But because this relation to God is perverted, it takes very strange forms. Luther says somewhere that man has either God or a caricature of God, God or an idol. God is one, but the idols are many and very varied. But an idol is always something unconditional, an absolute—something to which we know we are absolutely in thrall, something that possesses us not in a divine but in a demonic manner. In truth, Nietzsche, the enemy of Christ and an atheist, who called himself the anti-Christ, was not without relationship to God. His relationship was love perverted into hate, a demonic enmity to God and Christ which possessed him rather than his possessing it. Only at that point where man in complete stupidity and mental vacuity nears the boundaries of humanity, does the boundary of the relation to God also come in sight. Godlessness, sin, and even denial of God are not an absence of relation, but negative, perverted relation. This relation is ours up to the moment when God's Word again takes possession of us.

The second perversion is that of human nature itself. It shows itself in a contradiction. On the one side man is the being

created by God in his image, who carries inamissibly his eternal
destiny in himself, in his nature as a human being. On the
other side, he is the man who has missed this destiny, who
has determined himself in opposition to it. He is therefore in
contradiction to himself. Man is the only one among all the
creatures who lives in contradiction to himself. This contradiction
in his own being is characteristic not only of certain men, whom
we call especially inharmonious and divided personalities, but
of all, even those who are thought to be harmonious and inte-
grated. They all have the contradiction within them, or rather,
they all *are* in this contradiction.

Whether concealed and unconsciously, or openly and consciously, they are divided in themselves, not at peace with
themselves; they bear within themselves two mutually incompatible principles or laws of life, namely, the life-principle of
willing or desiring and the life-principle of the "ought." In this
"thou shalt," in this legalistic form of responsibility, the original
Word of God in which they were created manifests itself in
them. Even the sinful man, who has fallen from God's order
of creation, knows something of the divine will; he still knows
of a responsibility. But he knows of it only in this fragmentary
manner of the "thou shalt." He knows neither rightly what God's
will is, nor what the destiny of his life is. And above all, he
does not fulfill the destiny of his life. The law of his real being
is another than the law of the "ought": this dualism of "ought"
and "is," of ideal and reality, tears asunder the life of man; it
is unrest and the deepest cause of his lack of peace. The Apostle
Paul has given to it in the seventh chapter of the Epistle to
the Romans the classical expression for all time: "The good
that I would I do not: but the evil which I would not, that
I do."

The third perversion is that of the relation to our neighbor,
to our fellow creature. In the divine ordering this relation is
love, that we should be there for one another. But in reality
this relation is self-love; that is, the attitude of will and the
idea that the other is there for me. This seems an unjust and
hard judgment. Surely there is also much unselfishness and self-

sacrifice; it seems an exaggeration to assert that in reality men are simply self-seekers. It cannot be denied that there is much good will in the sense of moral goodness, in the sense of a certain civic ordinary righteousness, and in the sense of a certain conception of "the gentleman" or human benevolence. All this the Bible does not deny. But it certainly does deny that there are men in whom this love of their neighbors is the fundamental law of their lives, from which all their actions flow. This is just where the rift comes in, because what we ought to do—to love—is something different from what we really want to do. What we *really* seek for in the *last* resort is ourselves, our own happiness, honor, welfare, success, and so forth. This again cannot be proved, but it is confirmed by every man who honestly examines himself. Measured by the standard of absolute selflessness and love, everyone must say of himself, "It is not enough; the small amount of love that is in me is continually swamped and dominated by self-will. I love myself more than my neighbor. I love not God but myself with all my heart, and with all my soul, and with all my power. I am neighbor to myself."

4. *The Revolt Against God*

What then is the real man? Just this man, who is indeed responsible, but who, when measured by the law of responsibility, recognizes his failure, who is indeed destined for life in God's love but in reality is dominated by self-love, and therefore is living in conflict with God and himself and so is not at peace. Much more could be said about the manifestations of this unrest —about the longing, the anxiety, the insatiability of desire, the doubt and the despair. I must, however, content myself with this reference. We put therefore again the decisive question: "Is *this*

man the real man?" Can we see this picture set up before us; can
we identify ourselves with this picture?

I must return now briefly to the problem which formed our
point of departure: modern man. What in particular is there
to say about this so-called modern man? Obviously nothing that
would add a basically new characteristic to the picture of the
real man that we have sketched, but merely one or two words
which especially emphasize one trait or another in this picture.
In modern humanity there has been a specially conscious act
of emancipation of human self-will from the divine will. Modern
man has made a more open break with the divine authority,
he has asserted his self-dependence more decisively and unconditionally, than was ever the case previously. Modern man is
therefore, above all, emancipated man, man conscious of his
autonomy and proud of it. It was in the age of the Renaissance
that this man first took shape—the man who affirms what had
hitherto always somehow been described as sin, the man who
no longer acknowledges the concept of sin, the man whose own
will is his highest law, not only in practice but also in theory,
not only "unofficially" and tacitly but "officially" and explicitly.

The powerful lever which was used to bring about this liberation from subjection was the autonomous reason. By its means
man asserts his self-dependence, for by its means, as we said
at the beginning, he makes himself God. Rationalism in this
all-embracing sense, the declaration of the rational man's self-
independence, the proclamation of his coming of age and thus
of his independence of all authority and restraint in virtue of
his reason—this is the hallmark of modern humanity. Man seeks
the truth and the law in himself, in his rational nature. Opinions
may differ as to whether something divine manifests itself in
this inner law or not; as to whether this law of reason is in-
terpreted idealistically or naturalistically; as to whether it is in-
terpreted metaphysically with Kant, or whether with Nietzsche
the decisive break is made with all otherworldliness and so
with all metaphysics and religion. But that man bears the principle of his life within him, whether divine or not, that no
divinely commanding or divinely bestowing Thou confronts

him—precisely this is the common avowal of modern man, whether he belongs more to the idealistic or naturalistic or mystical-romantic type.

Thus the faith in the autonomy of reason confronts the faith in the bestowing and challenging will of the Creator. This is why modern man from the outset repudiates the idea of a speaking God who bestows life upon us in his Word and claims us for himself. And this not because it is unscientific, for neither the one faith nor the other is scientific, but because it is opposed to his autonomous self-will. Therefore the choice between the one and the other is not a matter of education or of reflection or of knowledge, but a matter of decision. Is man to acknowledge God as his master, or does he wish to remain his own master—that is the only issue at stake. And there at last all arguments cease, and nothing is left but a naked "Yes" or "No."

In conclusion let us follow a little further the possibility of this "Yes." In so doing we shall turn to the other task, which was sketched at the beginning, even if we do so only very briefly.

If one is an emancipated man, involved thus in the contradiction, how can one come to affirm one's faith in God, to acknowledge God as "my Lord"? This possibility certainly does not exist on our side. For we ourselves, the real men, have once for all broken with that original principle, the Word of the beginning. We have so broken with it that we not only no longer will it, but so that we no longer recognize it. When of ourselves we think of responsibility, we do not think of the bestowing, loving God, but at the highest we think of a divine law, a "thou shalt." But this is the end of what is possible to us. Further than this point—that we ought to do what is good but cannot—we do not come, according to the witness of the Apostle, which continually vindicates itself as the truth.

Through our emancipation from our original destiny, we have lost the connection with it; that is, it has become a different destiny to us. From being one of bestowal, it has become one of legal demand upon us, and this makes our situation hopeless. We cannot by fulfillment of the legal demand of the "thou

shalt" find our way back to the divine love—because we cannot
fulfill the demand. We remain forever the debtors to this claim.
We can never get back to the beginning. We remain from the
beginning severed by the break that has taken place. But now,
precisely at this place where we recognize the impossibility of
our return to the beginning, the Bible speaks to us of another
possibility, which certainly is not ours but God's: namely, that
the beginning should come back to us, that the Word of the
beginning in which we were created should bestow itself again
upon us after we have lost it. It is just of this divine return to
the beginning that the Bible speaks. It deals with this Word
of the beginning that returns to us, when it deals with Jesus
Christ. This is why it calls him the Word of God that was in
the beginning, of divine nature, the divine life and light for
all men. It says further that this Word of the beginning came
to men who had lost it, *dwelt* among them, that it was thus there
in the form of a *man*, as the incarnate Word, that became man
and history.

5. *Jesus Christ*

Once more—everything depends on this point—this Word is
none other than the Word of the beginning, the Word in which
we were created, to which we men even in our sin, unfaith,
and godlessness remain bound. We are told expressly, "He came
unto his own." He came to those who belonged to him from the
beginning. He came to them as the Word in which they were
created, and to whom therefore they remain responsible forever.
But—now he came to them, to us. The Word is now here in
another form, not in the form of the Word of creation but in
that of the Word of historical reconciliation and redemption;
that is, of the Word that brings back the lost beginning and
restores the broken connection. It is now there in a form which

at one and the same time restores the original beginning and
indicates what has happened in the interval. He came to us in
a lowly form answering to our society. This form is called Jesus
Christ, the crucified.

We must pay attention to both statements: that Jesus Christ
is *the Word,* and that the Word is *Jesus Christ.* He is the Word.
And this indicates that in him God speaks again to us; in his
speaking to us, and indeed in his speaking to us in love, we
have life. He gives back to us our lost life in God by speaking
to us again in love as at the beginning, but now in another
manner, in forgiving love. This Word spoken to us thus restores
our life again to the realm of our origin. We are challenged
to answer this Word. This life can only be given to those who
allow this Word to be spoken to them, who accept it, who
decisively say "Yes" to it. This is what the Bible calls "faith."
Faith as the human "Yes" to the divine love corresponds to the
divine Word. Through this faith the divine love becomes our
own. This is what happens in Christ.

But now the second point must be emphasized. This Word
is not simply a word in the grammatical sense. It is a Person,
a *personal life.* When God speaks with man, he does not merely
speak with him as we do, through language; he speaks through
deeds. And more, he speaks in such a manner that he himself
is present. God does not deliver a lecture to us, God speaks to
us. Speech goes from person to person. Speech means that one
who is present makes a claim upon you. This presence of God
in his speaking, this personal presence,* finds its expression in
the fact that it is a person—that it is Jesus Christ—in whom God
speaks to us, in whom he restores to us the Word of the beginning.

And therefore we can now also understand why and how
far the Bible is called God's Word. The true Word of God is
not the Bible but Jesus Christ. *Christus rex et dominus scrip-
turae.* The reformer Luther opposes all dead literalism with

---

* TRANSLATOR'S NOTE: Here there is an untranslatable pun in the German.
Dasein in German is a word that means personal being, but it also means
"being there"—or "presence."

"What deals with Christ, that is apostolic"; that is what is at stake. Not a separation between the two, but a clear and un-ambiguous subordination is made. We have not faith in a book, but faith in a Person. It is not a book that is our authority, but a Person; Christ himself is the Word.

But the book is the witness to this person, the witness to the Word that he is and will bestow upon us. In the Bible the fact and the person Jesus Christ is offered to us as word in the grammatical sense, as a report and as teaching. For it must come to this, otherwise we do not really understand. We can only understand what becomes word for us also in the grammatical sense. Music, for example, can only say God's Word to us when it is set to real grammatical words. This is the priority of words among all means of expression and communi-cation. When person communicates itself to person, there the means of the communication is the word.

The Bible is the original record that bears witness to the Word that is Jesus Christ as a historical phenomenon. It bears witness through recording what he said and did. And Jesus Christ is the Word of the beginning in whom we were created. So the one refers us back to the other. So the one is ground and criterion of the truth of the other. The Bible is divine truth because and in so far as it bears witness to Jesus Christ and shows him to us. Jesus Christ is divine authority, our Lord and Redeemer, in so far as he, this man, is the Word of the beginning, the eternal Logos, the eternal Son. Our faith is there-fore related to this Word in the Bible, not to the Bible as such. But we only have this Word in, with, and under the words of the Bible, even the *letters* of the Bible. We can distinguish between them, but not separate them. We have the Word of God through the word of Scripture, and in no other way, but we do not have the Word of God in Holy Scripture in such a way that it is at our disposal, but in such a way that we must repeatedly seek for it in Scripture. And we possess it only in so far as it possesses *us*, not our understanding, our knowledge, our thought merely, but our *person*.

The message of the Bible is not a theory about the origin

of the world, and not a report about historical events as such, but the call of our Creator and Lord, through which he wills to give us his love and his eternal life, and through which he calls us back into subjection to himself, out of the false usurped freedom through which we have become not really free but slaves of our own self-will and of the world. This message is clothed in a historical garment which often seems strange, foreign, and offensive to us modern men. For we are so often so much the captives of our own world of thought that we are not able to hear the eternal Word of God in this time-conditioned form. And we are so entangled in our autonomy that we use this time-bound form of the Bible as an excuse to escape from its claim. But the Church also, whose task should be to say to every age the Word of God about Jesus Christ which is given to it in the Bible in such a way that the Word can be understood, is often and repeatedly so poor and weak inwardly, and so lifeless, that it is unable to perform just this its most important task, and instead of the living Word of God, produces dead historical formulae, and is astonished when men hungry for actuality will not accept the formulae from it. Therefore it is not merely the unbelief of those without, but just as much the lifeless faith of those within, that is to blame for the vast chasm that yawns between these who affirm their faith in the Bible and those who will have nothing to do with it.

But the greatest obstacle to the penetration of the gospel of God is always set up when the people who confess their belief in this Word, by their life make this Word, which is a life-transforming Word, incredible and suspect, instead of awakening interest in this Word by the witness of their lives and opening men's hearts to it. For this reason the Word of God is itself always a judgment, not only on those who repudiate it, the autonomous, modern men who wish to remain their own masters; it is a judgment also on those who confess it and who in spite of their confession remain their own masters. The greatest obstacle to the effectual working of the Word of Jesus Christ is the Christian community itself. And therefore the first and most important effect of the Word of God in every age is to call the Churches—that is, those who confess themselves believers in this Word—to repent and take it more in earnest. To know what is God's Word, to have clear theological concepts, is one thing—and not an insignificant or unimportant thing—but it is not the thing that matters most. What matters is that Jesus Christ the Word of God should *become Lord* of man, and that men should not merely become his admiring panegyrists, eulogists, and exegetes, but his disciples and obedient servants. Without this reference even the best theological expositions must be described as misleading. The confession that Jesus Christ—that God—is our Master and not we ourselves, is only justified when this confession is honest; that is, when he really is our Lord. But in the moment when he really becomes our Lord, the autonomous humanity within us collapses. And this is the right relation between these two entities, between the Word of God and modern man.

II. FAITH IN THE CREATOR
AND THE SCIENTIFIC WORLD-PICTURE

1. The Attack of Science

In the year of 1647 there appeared in England a work on the chronology of the Old Testament, by a theologian of the Anglican Church, John Lightfoot, in which the well-known author communicated as the result of his investigations the information that man was created by the Trinity on the 23rd October, 4004 B.C., at nine o'clock in the morning. This exact dating of the work of creation may be a singular phenomenon, but a look at the standard commentaries on the book of Genesis from Augustine to Luther and Calvin shows us that all these Church teachers of earlier times did not only conceive of the story of creation in six days in a more or less literal fashion, but that they also believed in the possibility of fixing its date, even if perhaps not in so exact a manner, and that all churchmen until far into the eighteenth century held it as an indispensable article of faith of the Church that a few thousand years ago the world—just as it is today, together with its flora and fauna just as we know it today—was created.

How great the prestige of the Bible as a source of cosmographic information was, even well into modern times, can perhaps be seen most clearly from the fact that even geologists of the eighteenth century, who were already working with very modern scientific methods, had still no doubts about the fact of the flood as the Bible records it in its first chapters, just because it was recorded in the Bible. And so the Bible is still today for many the book that informs us when and how everything that exists came into being.

Therefore we understand how the clash between Christian

faith and modern natural science was bound to be an extremely
violent one, that a battle was joined which seemed to be a
matter of life and death. The first clash was connected with
the scientific achievement of Copernicus. Of this, Luther said:
"These fools wish to subvert the science of astronomy, but holy
scripture tells us that Joshua commanded the sun to stand still,
and not the earth," and Calvin condemned all who were not willing to believe that the earth is the central point of the universe.
The fate of Galileo and Giordano Bruno is known. And yet
the Church gradually reconciled itself to the teaching of Copernicus, even though slowly. The second big clash came from the
side of geology and biology. The names of Lyell and Darwin may
stand as representative here. The evolutionary picture of the
origin of the world of life took its rise, and gradually fitted
into a unity with the astronomical theories about the origin of
the universe. It is understandable that the conflict was sharpest
where man himself was concerned. That even man himself
should have developed from pre-human forms, that even he
should be fitted into his place in the continual process of becoming, all this seemed to stand in an irreconcilable contradiction with the central point of Christian faith, with the doctrine
of the state of original sinlessness in the Garden of Eden and
of the fall of man. It was either Christianity or Darwinism,
either belief in the creation or acceptance of the doctrine of
evolution.

In these struggles the Church proved to be the weaker of
the combatants all along the line. Though at first with difficulty
defending itself against Church opposition, science pressed re-
morselessly forward with more and more speed, against less
and less opposition as time went on, and conquered the terrain
of which for fifteen hundred years the biblical ecclesiastical view
had remained the master. Today the struggle has abated, but
not for wholly satisfactory reasons; very often the silence which
has here supervened means nothing more than that the forces
of the Church and those of the scientists have so far lost touch
that there is no more friction. We theologians tend easily to
undervalue these things; for the non-theologian or so-called lay-

man the question, belief in creation or in the scientific world-view, is of far more burning interest than most of the problems which we discuss when we get together. The situation, however, as a rule is this, that the layman sees himself confronted with the alternative, either scientific world-picture or Christian faith. That theology has done so little to help him to transcend this fatal alternative is a grave fault, and is one of the reasons why so many men today—I do not say educated men, for this scientific knowledge has long been shared by the elementary schools—turn away from Church teaching and from the Bible, because an interpretation was not offered them which is compatible with scientific knowledge.

This is all the more regrettable because this is not a real problem but only a sham problem. The conflict between natural science and biblical faith, wherever it breaks out, is always a sham problem; that is, a dilemma which is not rooted in the thing itself but in a false understanding of the thing on the one side or the other, or on both sides. Certainly the traditional form of Christian doctrine made the conflict inevitable. If biblical faith is necessarily linked with a definite world-picture, then either science must be subordinated to faith, or faith to science. That in the Bible there is to be found a definite world-picture is beyond question; that is, a definite view about the way the world and the bodies in it came into being, their age, extension, and mutual relations, and similarly with regard to the origin of life and man within the world thus conceived. It is equally beyond doubt that this world-picture is a quite different one from that of modern science. And lastly, no one who knows science can have any question as to which of the two world-pictures, the biblical one or the modern scientific one, is the one he must accept. None of us can any longer doubt that Copernicus was right—even if since his day the picture of world-space has grown a million times larger, and the old question as to whether the earth or the sun moves has become meaningless as a result of the theory of relativity. The old biblical world-picture has become forever a thing of the past, even if in a hundred years' time the scientific world-picture of today may seem just as hopelessly antiquated. Everywhere that science is studied the evolutionary theory too has won the day, although it has suffered various modifications, and the Church would do well simply to take notice of this fact. But in two directions the Church took its teaching task too little in earnest. First, it did not make clear enough that faith in the Bible does not as such imply the acceptance of the truth of every individual cosmological or historical statement in it; the old orthodox doctrine of verbal inspiration—that is, of the inerrancy of every single statement of Scripture—has dreadfully obstructed the access of the men of our time to the Bible, and here the word of Jesus against the scribes holds good, that they close the kingdom of God to men—this time through the mental sloth of their conservatism.

The doctrinaire obstinacy of the Church has here shown itself in a very shocking form. The doctrine of the literal inerrancy of these Scriptures—which the greatest Bible lover of our Church, Luther himself, expressly repudiated—places the Christian of today in an incurable conflict with science and thereby shatters the inner unity of his life. That this special orthodox doctrine is not identical with the biblical faith of which we have spoken is obvious. The claim that the Bible is *witness* to God's Word Jesus Christ, that consequently it is only God's Word in this indirect sense, by no means involves the assertion that all its particular statements are inerrant. On the contrary, Scripture is the cradle in which Christ lies, says Luther. Scripture shares in the human nature into which the Lord Jesus Christ came, and which he, the eternal Word of God, took upon him. To this human side of Scripture belongs above all its time-conditioned transitory world-picture.

This brings us to the second point. The Church has also failed in not recognizing, or not recognizing with the necessary speed and decisive clarity, that the world-picture of the Bible, even that part of it which concerns the creation of man, is such a time-bound element of Scripture. Nor did it make on its side the attempt to express the truths that were at stake in terms of the new time-scheme. The world-picture is, as it were, only the alphabet, the sound-material in which the Word of God is spoken. Just as it makes no difference to the meaning of the word "man" whether we say it in Greek or German or Finnish, and whether we write it in very large or very small letters, so it makes absolutely no difference whether we formulate it in the language of the ancient or modern scientific world-picture. Here, too, the Apostle Paul's word of warning holds good, "The letter killeth, but the spirit maketh alive." A rigid holding to the letter of the Bible—to the ancient world-picture, which is also that of the Bible—has indeed killed; that is, it has driven many people into a dilemma, in which in the end there was a conflict between honesty and faith. It is high time that we earnestly set about doing what is necessary to remove this false dilemma. The Church must not fight against science. Its battle lies in a quite different terrain. It is not modern science but modern man, the modern faith in the autonomy of reason, that is the enemy; not the evolutionary world-picture but the evolutionist philosophy.

But now we owe it to our readers to prove that the Christian belief in God the Creator, in the world as God's creation, in the creation of man in God's image, and in the fall of man from this divine order of creation—indeed, the substance of the Christian faith—can be apprehended in such a fashion that the ancient world-picture, both of the cosmos and of the creation and the being of man, which science has laid in ruins, no longer plays a part in it. We must accordingly find a form for the belief in creation at which the scientifically educated man as such can take no offense. This we can only succeed in doing if we are sufficiently acquainted with the results and methods of modern science, indeed if we are as much at home with this scientific thinking as the men of old time were with their old world-picture and their ancient cosmological categories.

This condition is indeed to a large measure fulfilled in everything that relates to the cosmos in the sense in which it is the object of astrophysics. We have become accustomed to the thought that the universe is a million times greater than the ancients conceived it to be. The astronomical numbers, where the inconceivable spatial concept of the light-year is the unit, where accordingly the distance between the sun and the earth no longer represents even a millimeter in the metrical system, terrify us no longer. We have become accustomed to them, just as to the racing speed of an express train. That the earth as a mass in this universe has no more significance, and has no claim to spatial distinctiveness any longer, because there are no longer any distinctive points at all, has equally become a commonplace to us. Space has indeed only a very remote relation to the contents of faith. It is otherwise with time. For the Christian faith is in its essence historical. Time plays a distinctive role in it. It is a staggering thought that our history, which we boldly call world-history, hardly counts as a second in the world-year of cosmic history. It is less than a world-second ago that the first culture took shape in the Nile Delta; it was only a few seconds ago that the first men—perhaps of the type Homo Sinanthropus or Pithekanthropus—came into existence. We see in the telescope events which took place at least a hundred million years ago, whose light-message is only reaching us now, because the distance is so incredibly great. But to conclude, what has quantity, what has the enlargement of the picture of space and time, to do with the thought that God is the Creator and Lord of the world? Why should we, because the world has become so much greater, find it more difficult to say this than the men of old time?

The serious difficulties only begin at the point where the question is raised about ourselves, about us men. And this in two respects. Can we today still take our fate as men so much in earnest, when it is a mere nothing in the universe? And can we still speak of man as a special creature of God when he is merely a link in the chain of the evolution of living creatures? What does "the image of God" and "the fall" signify in the scientific world-picture of the present?

2. *The Error of the Attack*

The first question is more quickly answered than the second. In principle it was first answered by Kant. Just as man as an object, as a piece of the spatial causal world, has diminished to the verge of comparative nothingness, as a subject he has become greater in the same degree. For this incredible extension of the picture of the universe is itself the product of his science, and thus of his mind. It is the mind of man that reckons the millions of light-years and measures the new world-horizon. The cosmic vertigo which in the new age has attacked man in relation to this infinity of the world, is not the product of the enlargement of the world but an event in the mind of man himself. Man has appeared to himself as nothing because he has lost the firm ground under his feet, because his faith in God has become insecure. A man who rejoices in his faith does not trouble his head because the earth is no longer in the middle of the universe. The history with which faith is concerned cannot be measured by the astronomical clock and the astronomical calendar of the universe. Today is no less God's day, and therefore the time of decision, because it represents a mere second in world chronology. It is not because the world has grown so great that man has lost his faith; but because man has lost his faith, the greatness of the world has become a cause of panic terror to him. The panic comes from within, not from without, from modern humanity, not from modern science.

The conflict between science and faith was at its height when Darwin's book *The Descent of Man* appeared, which threatened to destroy the central biblical doctrine of the image of God in man, his origin in creation, and his fall in sin. There were at that time plenty of theologians who threw up the sponge and in one way or another surrendered these central doctrines of the Christian faith. The need to discuss this question gives us an occasion to reformulate the doctrine of the image of God in man, his origin in creation, and his fall. One thing is clear: belief in the *historicity* of Adam and the Garden is just as much a thing of the past as the conception of the three-decker universe. However many steps in the scientifically constructed family tree of man may remain conjectural, the knowledge which we now have of the evolution of man from more primitive beginnings leaves no room for the story of the Garden which could have happened so many thousand years ago in this place or that—for example, in South Arabia or mid-Persia. This story about the origin and primitive times of man belongs, like the six-days work of creation, to the transitory and outdated world-picture of the Bible. What then remains? We answer, "Everything in which faith has an interest!" It is evident here, too, that the conflict between faith and science, wherever it may arise, is a sham problem that rests on a misunderstanding. In this misunderstanding usually both sides—the representatives of science and the representatives of Church doctrine—have a share. So is it here also.

We shall speak first of the misunderstanding on the part of science. It consists in the belief that the modern evolutionary theory has invalidated the conception of the singularity of man. Man, it is said, is "nothing more than" a mere highly developed animal. In this phrase "nothing more than" lies the fallacy. To show the gradual *genesis* of man from pre-human forms of evolution is not in the slightest degree to impugn the *singularity* of man. The gradual appearance of the singular does not mean that it is not singular. Even the ancients knew that the individual man is first an embryo in the womb, that he goes through stages in which he does not yet show any of the singular characteristics of humanity—indeed, that even the infant hardly of itself shows any manifestations of a singular being. Here the animal element is still completely predominant. Although they saw this, they knew that man is something singular; the singularity becomes finally evident, even if only after long development. The continuity of evolution does not exclude the discontinuity in the thing itself. However man in this way or that may have origi-

nated from animal precursors, man is something different from
an animal, certain though it is that he has much in common
with the animals—precisely as an animal is something different
from a plant, although animal and plant have much in common.
What distinguishes man from the animal is not his understanding, for animals also have understanding, even although it be in
a lesser degree. Nor is it the soul, for the animals also have
souls, even though they are of a different character. What fundamentally and sharply and unconditionally distinguishes man
from the animals is precisely what the Bible calls the distinctive
element in man: that he, he alone, is created in the image of
God; that he is the being that is related to God, that knows of
God and eternal things, that is moved and disturbed, made
happy and uneasy by them; that he is the responsible being,
that he is a person. Whatever a beast may be, it is never a
person; man, whatever else he may have in common with the
animals, is distinguished from them by the fact that he is a
person. This abyss is deeper than all other abysses, with one
exception—the abyss between the Creator person and the created
person, between the Creator and the creature in general.

God created man in his image, in the image of God created
he him. What man? You and me!

> For thou hast possessed my reins:
> Thou hast covered me in my mother's womb.
> I will praise thee; for I am fearfully and
>   wonderfully made:
> Marvellous are thy works;
> And that my soul knoweth right well.
> My substance was not hid from thee, when I was
>   made in secret . . .
> Thine eyes did see my substance . . .
> And in thy book all my members were written,
> Which in continuance were fashioned,
> When as yet there was none of them.

Thus the psalmist writes about his creation by the hand of
God. He knows about his natural origin, but he clearly distin-

guishes it from his creation, or rather, from what is called empirical and natural origination, which is seen by the eye of faith to be creation by the will and thought of God. Creation is not an event which took place so many thousands or millions of years ago; it is rather the mystery of the origin that lies behind everything that becomes visible in time, the boundary between time and eternity. Creation is the coming forth of the temporal out of eternity, from the will and thought of God. Therefore creation is something that cannot be written into world-history, not even as its first point. The psalmist describes himself as created by God. He does not say that he is descended from a primordial pair who were created by God, but he claims to be just as much created by God as were that Adam and Eve in whose historical existence he doubtless believed. In relation to the creation there is no difference here.

Therefore we, too, are created in the image of God. Every man is created in this image; this is what makes every man a man. To be created in the image of God is precisely the same thing as to be human, and to be human is exactly the same as to be created in the image of God. The Bible at least teaches nothing else than that every man is created in the image of God, and that precisely therein lies the singular excellence of human nature.

It was only later Church doctrine which through its concept of the fall of Adam and of inherited sin was compelled more or less to deny this faith that every man was created in the image of God. By so doing it surrendered the biblical view. We must reaffirm it.

Linking up with the New Testament, we have acknowledged the sense of this existence in God's image to be this: our nature as created in the Word of God which has become flesh in Jesus Christ. We are therefore not only created *in* the image, but also *for* the image; that is, with the destiny of answering in our own personal life, in our own responsible action, to the creative and summoning Word—thus of ourselves loving as God loves, "that we may be the children of our Father which is in heaven." This is the destiny for which every man was created.

And in this destiny given at creation lies the special characteristic of human existence.

Does it not then lie in the mind of man? Can we not then say that what distinguishes man from all other beings is his mind? That, too, is right, although not in the same sense as our formulation that the special characteristic of man is his personal being. The mind is, so to speak, the substratum of personal being, in a similar way as the soul or the psychical element is the substratum of mental acts. But what distinguishes the mental acts from the psychical element is always this: their relationship to truth, idea, norm, meaning; to something which lies outside the given world of nature, something not given, but unconditional, absolute, normative. The mere forming of images is psychical, but the act that grasps truth is mental. Mere desire is psychical, but the will that directs itself to the unconditionally good or significant is mental. Thus understood, certainly, mind is the thing that distinguishes man from the animals, the special characteristic of man, the *humanum*. But now the question is from what perspective this *humanum* is to be understood in its meaning and in its unity. What is it that makes man really human? Is it his genius, the creative character of his intellectual productions? In a certain sense, yes, inasmuch as only man is capable of this. But this creative power can just as well be used in the service of inhumanity as for humane ends; there is a devilish use of reason just as well as a genuinely human one. The truly human use, however, is one in tune with the divine calling to love; it is love itself. Genuine true humanity is not genius, mind as possibility, as power, but mind as a definite direction, namely, as that direction which we have recognized as the divine destiny for man. What makes the life of man genuinely human is not the measure of mental endowment, but the full measure of love. It is essentially for this that man was created; in this he fulfills his true being, his personal and corporate destiny. Where today we say "person," the Bible says "heart." The heart—not the feelings but the totality of man, the total act—is the decisive criterion of what is human.

3. Of Existence in the Image of God

It is for this reason that the image of God in man, however true it may be that every man is created in this image, is an ambiguous thing in every man. Will he indeed decide for the destiny for which he was intended? Will he love God with his whole heart, and his neighbor as himself? Will he fulfill the purpose of his being, and become thus a true, human, man? Will he act according to his responsibility, or will he fail in his responsibility? With responsibility freedom is given, freedom as possibility of saying "Yes" or "No," responsibility as the necessity of either saying "Yes" or "No." In being created in the image of God, man is created to make this decision. Indeed, in this decision is determined the nature of his incarnation—whether it is in a true or a false humanity. How then does it stand in relation to this decision? Here, at this point, the Bible sets beside the primal word "Creation" the second great word which is to describe the being of man: Sin. Man makes the wrong decision: instead of for God, against God; instead of for love of God and neighbor, for self-love; instead of for dependence upon God, for independence of God. This is the great "No" in the life and the being of man. We have spoken of this already, how this "No" brings a threefold perversion with it: a perversion of our relation to the Creator, a perversion of our human nature itself, and a perversion of our relation to our fellow creature. We have yet to speak of this perversion under another aspect.

We said: Every man is created in the image of God. Of what nature is this perversion? The judgment of the Bible is as follows: Just as every man is created in God's image, so every man has fallen from the destiny God planned for him, thus has fallen into the threefold perversion we mentioned. I speak of this event in the past tense. Why so? How has the Bible the right to say from the outset that this has happened to every man? With this we touch upon the second, the negative mystery of human nature, the counterpart to the positive mystery, that of creation in God's image. Here we have to do with those realities which the Church has tried to grasp by means of the concepts "fall" and "inherited sin." Since we have surrendered the historical account of Adam's and Eve's fall as *history*, what do we teach about the fall and original sin?

First the question: Why do we speak in the past tense? We wish to say by this means that for each of us the decision has already been made, and made in the negative sense. Every man who is honest with himself must confess the same: I am a sinner; that is, a man who loves himself more than he loves God and his neighbor. The decision has been made; that does not mean that it is not made again every day, but it means that when it is made every day it always springs from a decision that has already been taken. Why this is so, we do not know. All attempts to explain this miss the mark, particularly all evolutionistic attempts, which amount to this, that sin is in some way derived from some earlier stage of development. Sin as an act of decision cannot be derived in any such manner; by so explaining it, we deny its character as responsible act, and turn man from a subject into an object, a piece of the causal nexus. Sin as responsible act is inexplicable. One can indeed say it comes from arrogance, from unbelief, and so on, but all these are not explanations but definitions which bring into prominence the decisive element in the nature of sin. But if we say that sin comes from our sensuous nature, from the fact that we are not simply mind but also body, we falsify thereby the nature of sin. Sin as unbelief and lovelessness, as defiance of God and as self-will, has its origin not in our sensuous nature but in our mind, in our "heart"; it is personal act, not constitutional weakness. Sin is in its nature inexplicable.

And in the same way the origination of sin is inexplicable. We simply find it there; we see ourselves entangled in it—not through the fault of others but through our own—but in such a manner that this decision has always already been taken and it conditions our new decision in a negative sense. But there, too, we must give up a prejudice. It is not as if a decision of the past conditioned our present decision, otherwise we would not be actual sinners but, so to speak, the ruins of former sinners. No, we are *now* sinners; that is, the decision already taken is actual in every moment. We can perhaps best express it as Luther did: the person is sinful. This is what the doctrine of inherited sin is really trying to say. The total act which constitutes the person as a person is a negative act. But this total act is prolonged throughout our whole life. It manifests itself in our individual decisions, not as it would if there were no longer any decisions, but in such a manner that the decision which as individuals we make now is enclosed in a general decision which stamps its negative character upon the individual decision. This is the first point.

The other is perhaps even more puzzling. Of whom are we speaking? Of me, and of everyone. But how is it legitimate for me to speak about everyone, since I by no means know everyone? There might surely exist a man who is not a sinner. Answer: No. Just as all my individual decisions are encompassed by the original or negative fundamental decision, so all men are included in this one negative original decision. In this is manifested both the unity of the person and the unity of the human race. Whether the human race is biologically a unity or not is a matter of complete indifference, but it is a unity in its divinely ordered creation and destiny. Therefore it is also a unity in sin. The individual is bound together with his neighbor, we are a solidary whole, without prejudice to the fact that each of us is an independent person.

Perhaps we can most easily understand this by comparing it with its positive counterpart. Men are in a remarkable manner one, bound up in a unity and yet at the same time independent persons in the congregation of Jesus Christ. We shall speak of this later. In God's Word of creation, humanity is a unity in which one man is created and designated as a person actively and passively linked with another. This dependence on each other manifests itself in the world of experience with especial clarity in procreation and birth. Each of us came into being through two human beings who were our parents. And each of us through such procreation and birth owes his existence to many whom he does not know.

But now it is not right to identify this manifestation of the connection with the connection itself, as the Church doctrine of inherited sin did. By so doing, it introduced a naturalistic falsification of the concept of sin, and a disastrous determinism. It made man responsible for the sin of two persons which he really cannot help. By so doing it split up the concept of sin by distinguishing between actual sin and inherited sin, between sinful act and sinful inherited nature. The Bible itself does not do this. It does indeed acknowledge the inescapable power of sin over every single human being; it sees also the connection of this sin with the sequence of the generations; it refers accordingly, in consonance with its historical world-picture, to Adam's sin as the first beginning of this sequence, but in it we seek in vain for a doctrine of inherited sin. This was always read into it, and is not really to be read out of it.

For the Bible it is not the manner of the origin of sin that is important, but the *fact* and the *nature* of sin. It is the turning away of every individual from God and his neighbor. That is its nature. It is the self-determination of the will against God's ordering for us. It is never a state, but always an act. But it is at the same time an act that encloses and includes everything; it is a total act of the individual and a total act of humanity. It is something that man cannot avoid doing, and for which he is yet himself to blame when he does it. It is an act of freedom, and yet the man who does it is the slave of sin.

Both points are here asserted with equal energy: the responsibility, the character as act, that sin is always a personal and never a natural affair; and the inevitability of sin for the individual here and now, man's servitude to sin, the power of sin over his will. The Bible holds fast to this paradox. No one is held responsible for the guilt of another, and yet everyone is in solidary manner a sharer in the guilt of the sin of humanity. The story of Adam offered at first glance a welcome medium for the manifestation of this unity; the tracing back of the sin of the individual to this sin at the beginning was the more convincing because the experience of inherited character was universally known to ancient man. Therefore it was natural when, in opposition to the falsely rationalistic teaching of Pelagius, Augustine, the greatest teacher of the ancient Church, gave expression to the total character of sin in the form of the doctrine of inherited sin. But the Church paid dearly with this doctrine for victory over this form of liberalism. It did indeed assert the common responsibility of all men and so made impossible the pharisaic severance of the individual, by revealing his membership of a society fatefully involved in sin. But at the same time it gravely injured men's consciousness of responsibility, because the individual was accounted guilty of an act in which he had absolutely no part. The doctrine of inherited sin was a natural but not an unobjectionable first attempt to do justice to the solidarity of sin. This attempt has been made impossible by the scientific refutation of the Adam story. To the Church is given the task of reformulating the knowledge of the totality of sin. What has been offered here should be understood as an attempt in this direction.

Let us once more underline the decisive point. It is the attempt to affirm at one and the same time both the responsibility and the personal character of sin; that is, to assert that it is a real decision—this on the one hand, and, on the other, to affirm the element of totality. And this in a twofold sense, in the sense of personal totality—that man is a sinner—and in the sense of universality—that the whole of mankind is bound together in a solidary unity in sin, just as it is bound together in a solidary unity by the destiny of fellowship given to it by the Creator. We can put this also as follows: what we must do is to understand both sin and the origin of man as entirely personal, and at the same time entirely communal. For this is the basic thought of the biblical doctrine of man, that man is created in God's Word to be a personal and a social being.

4. The Destruction of the Image of God

In conclusion we shall again take a look at the question of the image of God. How do matters stand with it? Is man still a creature in God's image, or is he so no longer? This has been a very troublesome question for the Church to answer, and on the whole its answers have not been very happy. The problem that it had to solve is as follows: Are we to say that man as man is still in God's image? Then sin has changed nothing in his being, so sin cannot be so bad an affair. But if we say that man has lost the image of God through sin, then man is no longer man, or else there is a human nature without the image of God; that is, the image of God and human nature are torn apart. The ancient Church since Irenaeus found a temptingly slick formulation. Man, says Irenaeus, is created in God's image and in his likeness. The Bible uses two expressions. The image is what cannot be lost, but the likeness can be lost, and is lost through sin. What cannot be lost is human nature as such; what can be and is lost is the special gift of God's grace. This formula dominates the whole of patristic and scholastic thought. It is the basis of the whole Catholic system of nature and grace, of what has been admirably described as the two-story theory of Catholic culture, politics, and doctrine of the Church. But elegant as this solution to the problem may be, it is equally dangerous. For the nature of man is torn asunder; it consists in the first place of a part which cannot be lost, human nature, and second, of a part which can be lost, the divine gift of grace. Man's being is not solely based upon God's Word.

It was a tremendous achievement when Luther broke through this 1500-year-old tradition with his definition: the image of God in man is simply the life bestowed on him by God, his *justititia originalis*, his life in faith and love, in fellowship with

God. The image of God equals fellowship with God. But now Luther had his own difficulty in giving an answer to the question of what to make of the peculiar characteristic of human existence, the humanity which remains to man even in his sin, the quality that distinguishes him from an animal. Luther was clear about the significance of the question. He could not surrender the connection between human nature and the image of God, and so he taught that what still distinguishes man from the brute is a *relic* of the original image of God. But this formulation was clearly an attempt to extricate himself from an embarrassment. It imperiled the assertion that man had lost his original nature through sin, that sin is not a mere disturbance, but the destruction, of human nature. And so it is understandable that recently a further step has been taken, and it has been asserted that there is not even a relic of the image of God in fallen man. Sinful man has absolutely nothing of the image of God in him. But this means that for the first time in Christian history it has been denied that the human nature of man, in which even the sinner shares, has anything to do with the image of God. Man's nature, the *humanum,* has with this become a *profanum.*

In contrast with this, the conclusion of our representation is that the original nature of man is indeed completely perverted, that the relation to God and the relation to our neighbor have become thoroughly perverted, contrary to the purpose of creation, and inhuman, but that the relationship to God as such still remains, even in its perversion. The image of God in man is still there, but in perverted form; his knowledge about God is there, but in perverted form; his personal and communal existence is there, but in perverted form. Just as man is still a person, so he is still in a relation to God, he is still a responsible being. Man as a sinner does not stand outside of every relation to God, but he stands under the anger of God instead of his love, under law instead of under grace, in sin instead of in faith. Man is still, if I may say so, a theological being, but pervertedly theological, idolatrous, and demonic. Sin is no more profane than faith; but it is the perversion of something sacred. Therefore, even now, man is to be understood in terms of the image of God, but as the being that is in contradiction with itself, just as it lives in contradiction to God. Contradiction is something different from the absence of relationship. Even now man is entirely to be understood as God's image—but as his perverted image; the wine of God's love bestowed upon him has turned sour and become the vinegar of enmity to God. Sin is faith turned upside down, and can be understood in no other way. Even so, man remains a singular being; even sin, his perversion, is something that distinguishes him from every other creature. Man is the only being that sins: this is the greatness in his misery, which in the midst of his alienation from God betrays his divine origin. Man must be understood in terms of the contradiction between the divine image and sin, in terms of the contradiction between origin and fall. Precisely this, this contradiction between truth and falsehood in him, is the hallmark of the real man.

It is thus that the Bible understands man. It is wonderful how the biblical world-picture, outdated for us, has almost no effect on its understanding of man as creature and sinner. The impossibilities of the Church doctrine of the fall and inherited sin, which brings us into fatal conflict with science, are far from the Bible. It teaches exactly the same things about man that we, too, must teach: that man is God's image, but that this image is destroyed, and must be renewed. Man is completely a sinner, but this sin is not a condition but a determination of his being, and as such is an act, but an act that determines man as a whole. Therefore he is the slave of his own sin, and bound in a unity with the whole of mankind in it. There is no conflict between this doctrine of origin and sin, and the scientific knowledge of our day, unless science oversteps its limits and propounds some speculation of natural philosophy—for example, materialism or determinism—as scientific teaching. In that case, however, we have no longer to do with modern science but with modern man, who conceals his lust for autonomy behind the mask of science, and seeks to exculpate himself.

All understandings of man, with the exception of the Christian one, are attempts to exculpate man, but by exculpating man, they cheapen him at the same time, by robbing him of his personal character. Only the biblical understanding of man—the interpretation of him in terms of the Word of God that became flesh in Jesus Christ—does not exculpate him but condemns him. But in condemning, it maintains his personal character. And the Bible condemns him at the same moment as it acquits him of guilt. For the same Jesus Christ, the same Word of God in whom we know ourselves as sinners, is also the one who takes this sin from us.

III. JESUS CHRIST AND HISTORICAL LIFE

1. Bible and History

"When the fulness of the time was come, God sent forth his Son, made of a woman, made under the law." The Bible is distinguished from all other holy books of the world, by the significance which is given by it to the time factor. There is indeed mention in other religions also of special events in time, of very ancient times, and of the remote future; but behind these special times there is a background from which they only vaguely stand out, the background of timelessness. The individual historical events are only greater or less waves in the sea of unhistorical being, which after letting them tower up, engulfs them again within itself, so that after something has happened, everything is fundamentally just the same as before it happened. It is in the highest degree remarkable that the Greeks, whose incomparably fertile minds first raised most of the questions which today concern us, hardly ever reflected seriously about history. Their conception of the world, like that of all other pre-Christian peoples, is an essentially timeless one; historical events, to them, like everything that belongs to the world of becoming, are inessential, since only the timeless and eternal has essential significance. The myths also of the other peoples, even when they deal with apparently highly important events, betray their essentially unhistorical character by the fact that these highly important events recur continually. Adonis is continually dying and coming to life again; continually, after many hundreds or thousands of years, some incarnate deity comes and brings about a turning-point in world-history, which, because it is repeated in an infinite series, is no real turning-point. Here only the religion of Zoroaster is an exception. In it—outside of the Bible, for the first time—the idea of world-history, that is, the idea of a *unitary* history and a *historical* unity, appears. But this original religion of Zoroaster in its later development lost itself again in mythology, and that means in an essentially unhistorical kind of thinking.

In the Old Testament the historical character of religion is given from the outset by the fact that it is founded on a historical fact. The history of Israel begins with a determinate event, and with this same determinate event there begins also the religion of Israel. This event is the Mosaic revelation of God, or as the Bible itself names it, the covenant of God with the people of Israel through Moses the mediator of the divine Word to Israel, and the mediator of the answer of Israel to God. In him is fulfilled the communion between God and the people, and this communion is both the foundation of the religion and the foundation of the history of Israel. On this historical fact is built up the faith in God, the cultus, and the ethos of Israel, and it is the point on which everything turns. But now it is not as if this basic and primary fact of their beginning directed the gaze of this people backward. Precisely the opposite is the case; it is indeed the same God who has revealed himself there, who daily accompanies the people on its journey, helps it, and continually assures it of his revealing and saving presence, and—as we are told in the story of the Exodus from Egypt—goes before it in a pillar of fire. Thus this God gives to his people at the same time his presence and his future. The present life of Israelite man and the Israelite nation is strung between a definite, unique, and never-recurring past and an unambiguously definite future, which is thought of as definite and irreversible. The place of the mythical recurring cycle of all things has been taken by the extended straight line of time; time has gained an unambiguous meaning and an irreversible direction. What was, has been and does not come again; before is—irreversibly—before, and after is after; time is taken seriously. Something is being decided in time, and time is time of decision.

Even more clearly and comprehensively is this the case in the New Testament. The prospect widens from the history of one people to embrace humanity; indeed, the history of mankind widens to embrace the history of the universe in general. The danger was not slight that this double expansion of the historical horizon would lead to a blurring of this horizon, and its melting into an indeterminate eternity. The history of a nation is a sharply defined and definable entity; but a history of mankind, or even a history of the universe? We see in the example of the Stoic concept of humanity how destructively the idea of humanity and a cosmopolitan humanism can affect all sense of history. There is nothing so lacking in the sense of history as the thought of cosmopolitan humanism of late antiquity. But in the New Testament there is to be perceived nothing of such a regression to unhistorical timeless thinking. On the contrary, the time-factor is even more significant than in the Old Testament; time is still more radically understood as time of decision. The reason for this is the same event which is the foundation of the whole New Testament: the event Jesus Christ. "When the fulness of the time was come, God sent forth his Son, made of a woman, made under the law."

He was "made of a woman," he is a son of man; he is a truly historical personality, not a mythical or half-mythical figure. The chronicler knows of him that he is Jesus of Nazareth, son of David's descendant Joseph, the carpenter; a wandering preacher, a rabbi, and finally put to death by Roman justice as a Messianic claimant, "crucified under Pontius Pilate." We know of his brothers and sisters, and especially also of his mother Mary. If we are not in a position to write his biography, yet his portrait stands before us in the most full and natural visibility, delineated in detail before our eyes by trustworthy reporters. Even the unbelieving secular historian draws his human picture on the basis of what, after critical sifting of source material, remains at his disposal, in a manner not essentially different from that of the gospel of a St. Mark, although we grant that he omits that which is the central matter for the evangelist, the Messianic significance, the significance of the Christ. Even the man who wills to have nothing to do with Jesus Christ, cannot leave Jesus of Nazareth on one side. But the Bible claims that just this man, Jesus of Nazareth, is the Christ, the Son of God.

He was not only "made of a woman." He was "made under the law." By this law is meant his Mosaic inheritance. Jesus stands first and foremost in unbroken continuity with the revelation and story of Moses. He himself shares in this story; he is a true Israelite, a participant in this tradition of revelation, and precisely thereby "made under the law." As in the physical sense, so also in the historical and religious sense he is a son of Israel. He takes his stand consciously and unambiguously on the foundation of the Old Testament. Just as certainly as something new begins with him, so certainly this new thing does not signify a break in continuity. "I am not come to destroy, but to fulfil." The new thing in him is not something different. What is new in him is that it is only in him that the old receives its true meaning. He is the meaning, the content, the goal of the Old Testament, the Mosaic and prophetic revelation of God, and the history of the Covenant. He is the promised Messiah, the king, prophet, and priest in one person, and therefore neither prophet nor king nor priest in the previous, provisional sense. He it is in whom the lines of kingship, prophecy, and priesthood, never united in the Old Testament, come together, and by so doing obtain a new sense. This is the Messiah, the Christ, the vicegerent of God, the Son of the living God. This is what his disciple Peter calls him when he is the first man and the first disciple to express his faith in Jesus.

The title Messiah or Christ is an unambiguously historical predicate. In it at one and the same time a link is made with the past and our eyes are directed to the future. The Messiah is the One to whom the whole history of Israel is directed. The story from Moses onward runs toward the Messianic age; the Messiah and the Messianic kingdom is the positive content of the prophetic revelations. Messianic age, Messianic kingdom—this is God's kingdom among men, God's full presence among men, and men's full conjunction with God. All this is present in ancient Israel only in the form of suggestion, of preparation, and of prophecy. David, the true king of Israel, is indeed one who rules by authority of God and according to God's will—and yet he does not do this in the true sense; he is still too much his own master. The priest is indeed the one who reconciles men with God—and yet it happens in a remarkably inadequate, indeed misleading, manner. The prophet is indeed the one who speaks God's Word—and yet this is the Word of a distant God, and he who declares the Word is not he in whom God speaks as one present. Everything is, in a literal sense, pre-cursory. But now he himself, whose precursors and heralds they were, has come. The true king, the true priest, the true prophet—that is, the one in whom God really asserts his lordship, in whom he really reconciles the people to himself, priest and sacrifice in one, and he in whom the Word is present in person, in whom the God that speaks is himself here, Immanuel, God with us. What was previously merely here in *symbol*, is now here in *reality;* the meaning of the history of Israel is now come to her, while hitherto it was here merely in precursory form. The time is fulfilled—for God has sent his Son.

2. *Christ the Lord*

The Jews and Mohammedans have mocked at this idea that God, the almighty and exalted Lord of the world, should have a Son, "just as the fabled gods of the heathen have sons." They mean that in making this claim Christianity has fallen back from the stern monotheistic line, from belief in the exalted Lord God, to the level of the mythological heathen religions. And in fact the Christian message in the course of history has more than once been near to this danger of falling back into mythology. It is precisely for this reason that the doctrine of the triune God stands in the center of the Christian message. There is only one God, not two or three. But this one God, who created the world and sustains it, the eternal, inconceivable, mysterious One, the God who is concealed and inaccessible to our thought, has shown himself to us, has imparted to us his will, his nature, his love, and therewith himself. He has come out of his concealment—at first in a precursory foreshadowing, in the word of his prophets, and then finally in that Word which is not mere word, but the presence of the Speaker himself in that Word which is at the same time person, and that person who is at the same time God's Word.

This is the mystery of the person of Jesus Christ, that in him, this man, this carpenter's son, made of a woman, and made under the law, God himself is present. "God was in Christ, reconciling the world with himself." What we say about this—we theologians especially must be quite clear about it—is stammering. But even if it is stammering, yet it has a quite definite meaning: that this man, as well as being a man like us men—even if also a truly human man while we are always at the same time inhuman men—that he, this man who as man stands on *our* side confronting *God* as one who prays and worships, at the same time *confronts us*, as *God* confronts us, as one who gives to us who ask, what God alone can give to us; does to us what God alone can do to us; and says to us what God alone can say to us. And that everything that he says to us, does, and gives to us on the part of God, he does not say, do, and give as, for example, a prophet has done, for the prophet is in fact simply a man, only his Word is something superhuman, transcendent. But that Christ, the person who is identical with his Word, that he is himself this transcendent Word—that he, to say it once again, is himself the speaking Person of the present God—this is precisely what is meant. But how should we conceive of it, how is it possible that a man is at the same time God—this no one understands, not even a theologian. No apostle has ever claimed to understand this. The apostles—that is, the original witnesses to this Messiah Jesus, this Son of God—have simply described what we have also described, the personal presence of God in Jesus Christ, the unity of the human person with the Person of God.

We have no insight into the metaphysical possibility and nature of this existence, which is at the same time a divine personal and human existence. But we can and must say exactly what we mean by it, and why we speak thus. We can and should make clear to ourselves that it is only with this affirmation that the word *revelation* gets its full sense. If there is really revelation of God, if God's revelation as a perfect revelation is a reality, then it has this character, the presence of God himself with us. Only in a human person can God perfectly reveal himself, for only man is created in the image of God. Only a human person can really *say* something to us, only with a human person can we really have *fellowship*—not with something that is below this, nor with something that is above it. We cannot really have fellowship with the God who does not reveal himself to us in a human person, because he does not really encounter us. He remains at a distance, in a transcendence, which excludes real fellowship.

The same thing that is to be said from the viewpoint of *revelation* is to be said also from the viewpoint of *reconciliation* and *redemption*. The Old Testament, too, speaks of forgiveness of sin. But there this also remains something precursory. The weight of sin is not yet taken with full seriousness; that which lies between God and man is not yet disclosed in all its greatness. This only happens where it is shown to us how real is this obstacle that lies between us, so real that even God himself cannot simply ignore it. The expression of this negative reality, with which God's reconciling love must also reckon—this reality which cannot be canceled by a mere word, but only by a happening—is the cross of Jesus Christ as the event of reconciliation. It shows us that sin, the negative reality of our existence, proves itself active even at that point where God wishes to come near to the men who are separated from him, in true personal nearness like the personal nearness of one man to another. This nearness can only be achieved by means of this fearful event which is called the cross.

And third, the same thing that shows itself under the aspect of revelation and reconciliation shows itself also under the aspect of *redemption*. Redemption means not only redemption from the guilt of sin—this side of redemption is what we call reconciliation—but also redemption and liberation from the domination of sin, through the restoration of the unity of will between

God and man. For sin is the conflict of wills between the creature and the Creator, and redemption is therefore the removal of this conflict of wills, the restoration of the unity of wills. Admittedly not only this, but at the same time the removal of all that is a consequence of the conflict of wills and as a destructive sequel burdens human existence, darkens it, and delivers it to death. But the center of redemption is the center of the conflict, and this is the human will, the power of sin, not merely as an individual power but as one in which—as we have already seen—mankind is bound together as a unity and as a whole.

The power of evil also cannot otherwise be broken than by God himself drawing to himself, seizing and binding to himself, man who has withdrawn from him. And this, too, the distant God cannot do in his remoteness, but only in his personal nearness, as one who comes so near to us as only a man can come near to us. Indeed he comes near to us *in* a man, as himself, and makes us, as disciples of this Master, his obedient instruments, not by violence, nor by psychical compulsion, but in freedom. The only possibility of making another obedient in freedom is love, and, indeed, divine love, for every other love makes us unfree. But God can only show us divine love in *that* love which we are able to grasp, in perfect human love. Thus God overcomes the opposition of our will, through the power of his love in Jesus Christ.

But now everything that has been said is liable to a misunderstanding, which might rob us of the whole profit of our knowledge. The reference to the historical personality of Jesus of Nazareth, and of the Divine Person that in him, this human person, reveals himself to us, reconciles us, and redeems us, does not lead us to a historicizing misunderstanding, on one condition only, that we at once add this qualification: the historical Jesus is at the same time the present Jesus. Through the cross of Jesus we come into a real, immediate, vital relation with the risen Christ, and only where this happens is Jesus the crucified really for us the Son of the living God. The historical Jesus Christ is a mere useless memory if he is not the living Lord present with us, who has promised to his disciples, "Lo,

I am with you always." It is only the witness to the living, present, risen Lord which completes the message of the revelation, reconciliation, and redemption that took place in Jesus Christ. Therefore we do not speak of a God who is two-in-one, but of a triune God; Jesus Christ is present to us through the Holy Spirit. We have not to do with a historical report which as such has significance for us; we have to do with the God who encountered us there in the historical person Jesus, and encounters us here and now through his Spirit as the personally present power of God. We have not a historical God, not a God in a book, not a God who once in earlier days did something decisive for us, but a present God who, through what he did then does something to every one of us today; who, through what he then said, today wills to speak his word to the present life of each of us. And with this we are referred once again to the problem of time and of history. We have still the obligation to show in more detail how far in the New Testament historical time is still more seriously taken as time of decision than it was in the Old Testament. And this we must now discuss.

3. Of the Problem of Time

Time is for us finite creatures divided into these three moments, intimately interconnected with each other and yet fundamentally distinct: the past, the present, and the future. To take time seriously would thus mean to take each of these three, and each of them in its fundamental difference from the others, seriously; to take the past utterly seriously as the past, and the present as the present, and the future as the future, likewise. My thesis is that this has only been done and is done in the New Testament, through the message of Jesus Christ. Only through him does the past become genuinely the past, the pres-

ent the present, and the future the future. Only through him
are these three disclosed in their interconnection in our life.

The singular thing about the past is that it is unalterable.
What is past is unalterably settled; as past event, life has been
stamped with the rigidity of the immutable. It has been thrown
out of the stream of events, and deposited from it as no longer
fluid, as sediment. Even our past has this character; there is
indeed a past which is always with us, which always continues
to influence our life. That is not the real, true past. And conversely there is a past which is separable from us, which has
departed entirely from our life. But what then is that past which
is entirely past—that is to say, is unalterable and yet has not
departed from us but still belongs to us? This is guilt.

It did not necessarily need to be guilt; it might just as well
have been merit, the memory of our good deeds. But now in
fact it is guilt. Thus it is shown to us by the Word of God
in Jesus Christ. Our past is present to us as guilt, but present
in such a way that it is unalterable. To take the past seriously
is to take guilt seriously. Now this is the point in which the
biblical and especially the New Testament teaching differs most
obviously from all other teaching, the in-finite weight of guilt.
It has this weight because the relation between God and man
is taken with absolute seriousness as a personal one. By setting
himself against the divine will, man incurs irrevocable guilt, the
original relationship to God is destroyed. The present relation to
God is characterized by guilt as separation instead of by fellowship; as the contrary of fellowship, as enmity. And this guilt
is fixed in its immutability by being preserved from oblivion.
It does not pass out of date. God's books do not turn yellow
through age; the relation between God and man is seen to be
an eternal one. Thus his guilt also is eternal. Thus the separation
is also eternal. To be eternally separated from God, from whom
to all eternity one never gets free, this is hell. We said above
how in the message of the cross this guilt is taken seriously.
Not even God can simply set aside this negative reality—otherwise he would set aside the seriousness which his Word actually
creates. It is remarkable how easily most religions get around

guilt, and even more astonishing how lightly philosophers and
rationalistically emancipated men get around it. They do not
think that they are responsible for the past, or they do not
believe in its irrevocability. The past is not taken seriously as
the past, as my past. Here is the greatest conflict between the
Bible and modern man. Modern man does not take guilt in
earnest; the Bible takes it in dreadful earnest. Thus modern
man does not take his past in earnest; the Bible takes it in
dreadful earnest. And indeed this happens at the very point
where guilt is canceled out, in forgiveness through the cross of
Jesus Christ. That the removal of this past that separates us from
God "costs" no less than this: this shows with what absolute
seriousness guilt is treated.

The second moment of time is the present. Here it seems that
the non-Christian modern man has his special strength. He is
not much concerned with the past, and perhaps not much with
the future either; he is, as he says, entirely a man of the present.
But the three dimensions of time form an inseparable unity,
and he who does not take one seriously cannot take another
seriously. The man who is emancipated from God has absolutely no present. Precisely this is his trouble. He can never
say to the present moment, "Stay awhile, thou art so fair." He
is driven from what he has to what he has not, he is a perpetual
fugitive, he is afraid of time, he cannot endure it, he must—as
the phrase puts it with wonderful insight—"while it away." He
cannot quietly devote himself to the present. What is the great
sickness of modern men? That they—as we again say profoundly
—"have no time." They have time for nothing, for in the moment
in which they are living they are already thinking of the time
in which they are not yet, or of the time in which they no
longer are. They are sad or anxious, they escape from themselves
into the memory of past days, or they are anxious about the
future. They cannot truly accept the presence of the present.
They do not have the inner rest to do this—"the peace of God
which passeth all understanding."

What is the true present? What else can the true present
be but that which is true life, namely, love to God and our

fellow creatures? The man who lives in love is in the present;*
he lives with the man with whom he is, without inwardly trying
to escape from him. He bears with the other man, he gives
himself entirely to him in sympathy and helpfulness. He is there
to help him. This is the language of love: "I am here to help
you." Put negatively, love is not anxious. This is why Jesus lays
so much weight on freedom from care. Anxiety is a false way
of living in the future. Anxiety is the inability to live in the
present which results from not being united to God by faith.
The man who is united to God is carefree, for God cares for
him. He works—indeed, he plans also, he sees into the future—
but all these things do not fill him with care. Love is carefree,
it lives in the present.

Nor is love anxious about the past. It does not grieve over
what is past. "I forget what is behind," says Paul. How is this
possible after what we said about guilt? Answer: The guilt is
covered, canceled by forgiveness; the bond which was a deadly
burden upon us is, as Paul said, fastened to the cross, and thereby
annulled. And it is precisely from this forgiveness that there
springs the fruit of joyfulness in the present and freedom for
others. The burden of our own life is taken from us, and we
now have freedom to help our fellow men. Forgiveness of sins
makes men who are free and glad in the present, men who
live and sing in God's love as the larch tree grows and sings
in the sunlight. This is the note of triumph in the present which
we hear resounding through the whole of the New Testament,
but particularly clearly in the eighth chapter of the Letter to
the Romans. The past, which is recognized in all its gravity,
and acknowledged in all its gruesomeness as ours, is canceled.

How is it with the future? The future is the third dimension
of human time. But in a particular sense it is the first, decisive
dimension, which dominates everything. In order to live, man
must have a future. The man who has no future is lost. The
future is for the soul of man what oxygen is to the lungs.
The man who has no future suffocates. If we take the future

---

* TRANSLATOR'S NOTE: An untranslatable word-play in the German. The
word *gegenwärtig* means here both "present" and "in the present."

from a man, we kill him. It is just this that happens to the
man who is cut adrift from God, and in particular to modern
man. He has no future. He sees nothing before him but meaningless nothingness. Perhaps he has a future for tomorrow and the
day after, but it is impossible to keep one's eyes fixed arbi-
trarily on tomorrow and the day after. Man is made for eternity;
he must look beyond tomorrow and the day after, toward what
lies beyond them. And what lies beyond is death. The man who
lives unto death lives in a future that is no future. For to say
that "death is the end" means that there is no future for us.
The future has been cut off from us. The man who thus lives
unto death as his future is a man in despair. He has no oxygen,
he must suffocate. Therefore he must as it were seek for arti-
ficial respiration; he dare not think of death, he could not endure
it. He must hide his future from himself because it is no future.
Therefore he must always be seeking for new distraction and
diversion. Contemporary man's hunger for pleasure is the sign
of his latent despair. This is the way men act who have no
future, despairing men.

But the message about Jesus Christ gives man future. Not
merely "a future," as the Mohammedan religion gives its believers "a future" in their sensuously pictured paradise—but *the*
future, that is, the only future that is worthy of this name in
the radical sense of the word. This future is the kingdom of
God, the reign of God, eternal life in fellowship with the
Creator and every creature in love. The fulfillment of the life
for which we were created. The consummation of the divine
image. Jesus Christ is the bringer of this future, therefore he is
the Messiah. The man who lives through faith in Jesus Christ
lives in this future; he lives for this future and from this
future. He belongs to the world of the future. Therefore his
life is, as it were, ambiguous. He lives indeed, as we have heard,
in the present, because he lives in God's love. But he lives in
this present as one who is still only hurrying toward the true
fulfillment, the consummation of this present: "reaching forth
unto those things which are before."

The guilt of sin is indeed forgiven, and the power of sin

broken. Jesus Christ is indeed present, and with him eternal life. But it is only a beginning of this new existence that is here. Even as believers we are still sinners; the old man—that is, the old mode of existence—is indeed overcome in principle, but in fact the realization of this victory is only begun.

The Christian is one who waits, and hopes. But his waiting and hoping is different from what is normally so called, in respect of this, that it is not *his* hope, something therefore quite uncertain and in addition limited, but God's promise, therefore something all-embracing and fully certain. Faith is the firm certainty of things hoped for—as the Letter to the Hebrews says. The Christian has a future because he waits for the eternal kingdom as a certainty, indeed, lives already in it as something to come. He lives in his future. But he does not because of this become withdrawn from the present. On the contrary, it is only he who is living in the present—at least if he is a believer in the New Testament sense. For his hope cannot and may not withdraw him from what is already eternal life in its beginnings—from love. And the man who lives in love, lives in the present.

Thus in this way, through *faith* in the forgiveness of guilt, through *love* to our neighbor in which the divine love which is bestowed upon us expresses itself, and through *hope* in the coming kingdom of the consummation of love and of eternal life, each of the three dimensions of time—past, present, and future—in its own peculiar way is taken radically in earnest and they are conjoined together in an inconceivable manner. The same Christ who uncovers our past to us as eternal guilt, covers it also for us and makes us free of it. He translates us into God's love and makes us free for our fellow men, and thereby fully present. He opens before us the perspectives of the perfected eternal world of fellowship with God and man. He alone can say in more than an empty phrase, "We bid you to hope." He alone gives to us—in the full sense of the word—a future. And thus he fulfills the time.

4. *The Turning Point of the Ages*

There still remains one matter to be mentioned before we can fully understand how it is only through Jesus Christ that historical time is taken completely in earnest. The Bible does not say that Jesus fulfills the time, but that when the fullness of the time was come, God sent forth his Son. Thus in a unique manner eternity, time, and history are bound up together.

We must allow ourselves to be raised to an incomparable height rightly to understand the meaning of historical time or the historical character of time. We must ascend to the last summit to which the Bible gives us access, to what it calls God's eternal decree, revealed as the mystery of the Triune God, and revealed through Jesus Christ.

As the Mosaic revelation showed the divine meaning of history, this divine history was something which at a definite time—namely, the time of Moses—as it were broke into current history, a piece of divine history in the midst of this temporal world. But Paul shows us in his word something different. Time as a whole, the whole of temporality, so to speak, unfolds from eternity; time is released from eternity in order to return to eternity. Time as a whole, the whole of temporality, has this meaning and foundation in God's eternal will. The whole of history, not only a special salvation-history, has this eternal origin and this eternal goal. As the whole creation springs from the thought and will of God, so also does the whole of history. Not, indeed, as in the Hegelian philosophy of history, where history is simply the concrete unfolding of the divine idea, for the consequence of this Hegelian conception of history is that the series of historical events as such has in fact no significance. It is a strange duplicate of the eternal meaning; nothing happens in history that is not in truth complete beforehand. History then appears like a curtain unrolled from above, in which all historical figures are already inwoven complete, so that they are unrolled as thus complete before our sight in time. Thus history becomes an appearance; there are no real events there because there is no real decision there.

The New Testament picture of history is precisely the contrary of this. Here also the eternal will and plan of God is the theme, but not in such a way that time, the historical series, is devaluated. Here the *decision* is made *in* history. Jesus Christ is therefore the *fullness* of the time because in him occurs the *turning point* of the ages. It is not taught that history itself discloses step by step its eternal, divine meaning in a process of continual advance—as in the Hegelian philosphy of history—but rather that into history with its madness and absurdity, into this kingdom of darkness, there breaks, in Jesus Christ, the eternal divine meaning of world history. In battle with the meaninglessness and absurdity of the world of darkness and slavery, God reveals and bestows the new life, the eternal kingdom, the divine freedom, the divine love. The cross is the sign of this struggle and the sign that the victory in struggle is a deeply hidden and not a palpable one. It is the world of the resurrection that here breaks through into the world of death, but before the resurrection stands the cross, and only in the darkness of the cross can the light of the resurrection be seen. The meaning of history can only be revealed when at the same time the meaninglessness of history—the evil, the sin, the power of death, the kingdom of darkness—is revealed.

Here the decision is made, namely, the decision between death and life, between eternal death and eternal life, and between heaven and hell. *This* is the decision with which we have to do, in comparison with which every other decision is trifling. *This* is the decision which alone deserves the name of decision in the profoundest sense of the word. It is therefore *the* decision which either is never, or only once, made. The Christ event is the unique event that has once for all happened —the only event that can happen once for all, the turning point of the world, the reconciliation and redemption of the world.

Eph hapax, says the Bible itself: once and for all this has happened. For "the death that Christ died, he died once and for all." There are not two reconciliations and redemptions of the world. Either it has happened—then forever and eternally—or it has not happened. Everything that in other contexts is called a decisive event, compared with this is not a decisive event but an episode. Jesus Christ is not an episode but the fullness of the times, because he is the turning point of the ages.

5. *The Time of Decision*

Therefore it is only through Jesus Christ that historical existence becomes decision for every individual. Christian faith is nothing else than being enfolded in the decision which has been taken in Jesus Christ. This is what the act of baptism means: with Christ crucified, with Christ risen. A disciple of Christ is a man whose life henceforward runs its course as this decision, this turning point, as this struggle and victory. Faith itself is a decision. It is the contrary of a world view, a theory. There is no Christian world view; there is only a Christian decision, which consists in our surrendering lordship over our own life and placing ourselves completely under the lordship of Christ. What is at stake in Christian faith is the surrender of our right to property in ourselves, and the complete surrender to God's property rights. "Slave of Jesus Christ" is the Apostle's favorite title for himself. It is not a matter of assent to a particular doctrine, not correct ideas, so-called dogmas; in the Bible, as we have already said, everything is personal. What is at stake is that I should place my person completely under the lordship of the person of God, as he apprehends me in the person of Christ, through my acknowledging that God's hand in Christ is grasping for me. To let myself be grasped by this hand, and henceforward to will to be merely an instrument in this hand—that is Christian faith. And this is the issue here.

Faith can be said to be a change of hands, a property transaction. The man who was his own master becomes again what he originally was: God's property; the emancipated man returns to the hand of God, the Father and Lord; the prodigal son, who longed to be free, and came to grief in this freedom, returns to the Father and knows that he has been received again into the fellowship of the divine household. This turning back, which is at the same time a turning away and a turning toward, constitutes faith. This turning back, turning away, and turning toward is the complete reversal of the direction of life. All other decisions that we make are not really decisions, for in principle everything still remains as it was. It is only when we make this decision that nothing can remain as it was. "If any man be in Christ, he is a new creature: old things are passed away; behold, all things are become new."

This decision is on one occasion made for the first time, but from that moment it is a continual decision. It is now the hallmark of the man's life. The life of a Christian is one of ever-renewed turning back, turning away, and turning toward; the ever-renewed struggle, but the struggle that has its source in a victory already won, namely, the victory of Christ. This victory is threefold: the victory that makes my past free from the burden of guilt; the victory that makes my present free from the power of sin; the victory that makes my future free from care, anxiety, and despair, and opens up the way to eternal fulfillment. Thus the work of Christ has a threefold character: he is the priest who atones for guilt, the king who exercises the lordship of God, and the prophet who opens the future.

This means that the existence of every man—that is, of every believer—is given a new horizon in world history. Every individual Christian has a share in that decision which once and for all was made for the whole world, for all times, and for all the future, indeed, for eternity. The beginning in the eternity of God and the end in the eternity of God are thus linked together by what happened in the middle of time, at the turning point of the ages. The beginning of all is the eternal decree—

every believer knows that he was chosen from eternity; the end of the ages is the kingdom of God, for which everyone who believes knows he has been destined, called, and designated. But in neither case has it been through a mechanically unfolding history, but by reason of the decision that was made at that time and in his life is daily renewed. Only in this decisive manner can we share in the meaning of world history which Jesus Christ disclosed and bestows. Admittedly, even the unbeliever has a share in it. He, too, is placed before the decision, and even his refusal is a decisive one, decisive in the same manner as the "Yes" of the man who believes. The "No" is the decision for death, for the radical meaninglessness of life, as the "Yes" is the decision for life, the achievement of absolute meaning. Even for the unbeliever, Jesus is the point of decision—even where a man believes that he can avoid this decision. Since Jesus Christ, neutrality is no longer possible. Every man must decide for or against him; postponement is also a decision—a negative one. Here the reverse of what happens in politics holds good—empty voting-papers are counted as "Noes." "He that is not for me is against me." Thus Jesus Christ has made history the place of inevitable decision, and by so doing has given it for the first time its fully historical character. Only since Jesus Christ can we say, "It is high time." That for every man who has not yet decided, it is high time to decide rightly: this is the relationship between Jesus Christ and the historical existence of man.

IV. THE BODY OF CHRIST
AND THE PROBLEM OF FELLOWSHIP

The problem of fellowship is not one human problem among many others. It is *the* problem which thrusts itself upon us as the true problem in human life. There are certainly many other things in life with which man must trouble himself, and from which he can so often get no release—such as sickness, death, and physical and psychological suffering, which are connected with sickness and death. Let us provisionally call these problems the problems of destiny, these ills that assault man, coming not from man but from the extra-human reality. But nothing that comes upon man in this manner—for reasons which we shall later understand more clearly—has, in the first place, the bitterness that belongs to the evils that men do to each other, and, second, it is a fact that in most cases here also the sharpness of suffering is aggravated by intro-human relationships, and that, on the other hand, our suffering at the hands of fate almost or entirely disappears when the relationships between human beings is set in order. But what causes suffering between one man and another, and is felt as a problem, is in the last resort always the same thing, that men do not understand each other, that they work against each other, that one man, one group, one nation or race, seeks to oppress or exploit another. The great questions of the present which give us most trouble are all of this kind: the struggle of the nations for a place in the sun, the struggle of the races for equality or domination, the struggle of the classes for an equality in property or for privileges which have accrued in the course of history. And from these problems are derived their present aggravations in questions like war and peace, world war and world peace, communism and fascism, revolution, economic crisis, unemployment, to mention only a few. These are all problems which arise from the defective ordering of human fellowship. It is said, for example, quite superficially, that the world economic crisis arises from an overdevelopment of machine technology. From the viewpoint of political economy, this may be quite right—I do not venture to pass a judgment on this point—but we are too apt to forget that there is no such thing as technical overdevelopment as soon as humanity is an organism that is functioning rightly. There has never yet been too much production, but always too little. But, thanks to the bad organization of humanity, what is produced cannot reach those who need it. Exchange of goods is blocked, the arteries of mankind which ought to ensure the circulation of the blood are calcified, and the blockages are what we call a crisis. Thus behind crises, just as behind wars and revolutions, there stands the problem of fellowship.

Precisely the same thing that holds good on the large scale of the affairs which fill the political press, holds good of the affairs which are the theme of our daily talk, the so-called small things, which are much more troublesome to mankind than the so-called great affairs; for example, the marriage problem and the family problem. How large is the percentage of happy marriages in any town in comparison with the less happy ones, and with those which are nearly or totally shipwrecked? How many of those who read this are there who are not oppressed by wrong relationships between parents and children, or brothers and sisters, or whose life is not really embittered or crippled by such things? Again, the purely personal relationships between officials and their employers, between one colleague and another—what an unspeakable quantity of suffering, of silent but passionate conflict, how much hatred and bitterness, how much despair and feeling of the meaninglessness of existence, attaches itself to these relationships! When we reflect that all this would be unnecessary if men understood how to keep in fellowship with each other, but that this only exists because men do not live in true fellowship, then it is hardly likely that anyone will cavil when I repeat, that the problem of fellowship is *the* human problem.

1. Love and Life in Fellowship

This, too, is the view that the Bible takes throughout. It is, in fact, the Christian message, which shifts the problem of fellowship in this manner right into the focus of interest. Fellowship in human existence is simply love, love of our neighbor. To live in love and to live in fellowship are one and the same thing. When the Bible declares that love is the fulfillment of all the commandments, it claims that the problem of fellowship is the true, the central, and in the last resort the only problem of life. If men lived in love—in that love of which the New Testament speaks—then human life would be absolutely in order. Then the meaning of life would be fulfilled.

In no other religion is love—that is, fellowship—made central in this manner; in no other is evil so straightforwardly identified with lack of fellowship or opposition to it—that is, with love-lessness—as in the New Testament. Nearly everywhere outside of the biblical world, the sensuous nature, natural desire, the instinct connected with physical life, is looked upon as the true source of evil. But the Bible knows only this one simple antithesis: Love = the good; lovelessness = the evil. Love = life as human, true, and therefore happy. Lovelessness = life as in-human, untrue, perverted, blighted, and therefore unhappy.

The antithesis of love, and thus of fellowship, can indeed take very different forms. It can be present in the form of in-difference and complete lack of relationship. People take no concern for each other; we say, "They couldn't care less for each other." People live in worlds that never meet, just as the priest and the Levite went past the man robbed and left half-dead by brigands, a crass but in many cases unconscious form of lovelessness. Or it manifests itself in a mutual incomprehension.

It is easy to make the mistaken inference that here we have to do with an intellectual failure. In reality, incomprehension is always a failure in sympathy, a failure in the good will that listens to the other man and is there to help him. There may be a residue of mutual incomprehension which cannot be thus explained, but this incomprehension between men who live together in love is harmless, and does no hurt. The commonest form of lack of fellowship is more or less blatant egoism, ranging from slight feelings of unconfessed jealousy and the desire for the enjoyment and possession of one another, to cold, ruthless exploitation and enslavement, where one human being is made an object by another in the most brutal fashion.

The nature of love and fellowship is again made clear to us in the light of the denial of it. While we take it for granted that man has a dominating, objective, or exploiting relationship to things—for things are man's objects which he has at his disposal, which he uses and manipulates at his pleasure to further his existence—the same man, when he is confronted by another man, is faced by the question of whether or not he wishes to use the other man as an object also, and whether he has the right to do so, since the other man too, just as much as himself, is a subject, a self that does not wish to be treated like an object. It can now happen that the two of them come to an agreement with each other, that they divide, as it were, in equal portions between them the world of things in their area, and that each of them respects the other in the sphere thus delimited. Thus there comes into existence the regulation of egoism through law, resulting, provided that this acknowledgment is inwardly accepted, in justice—justice and the reverence for the other man, who is a subject just like myself, which is basic to justice. The acknowledgment of the other man as a possessor of the same reason as myself is the first breach made in egoism, and thus the first form of fellowship among men.

It is no small achievement when the relationships of men are regulated by law; but such a state of affairs is only outwardly different from that of egoistic anarchy, from the law of the mailed fist, where all are at war with all. The order that has come into being is only external, for the sake of the advantage that both parties reap from it. There is no inner transcendence of egoism. But where the relationships of men are regulated by justice, where men really reverence each other, there egoism is powerfully checked inwardly as well as outwardly.

And yet this cannot be called real fellowship. We must indeed in many interpersonal relationships be glad when at least the stage is reached where men deal with each other according to the rule of justice, and with a genuine desire for justice. In many relationships this is a maximum which we shall never do more than remotely approach, as for example, in the relationships between peoples, or between classes and races— indeed, in all collective relationships. The principle of justice is the only possible one for the regulation of collective relationships, because in all collectives an abstract, general regulation is necessary. Such a regulation can only follow the principle of utility or the principle of justice. Therefore there is indeed no true fellowship between collectives, but only—at the best— justice.

True fellowship comes into being only where I meet the other man as a Thou, whom I freely choose to help. Here we have a relationship of a wholly different kind from that in the case of justice. What holds good here is not the abstract principle "equality of all"; the individual is not regarded merely as the possessor of the same reason that is also in me. Here we have to do with the concrete, individual Thou in his particularity and—as we say—in his accidental givenness. To understand, acknowledge, and affirm this Thou in his particularity, in his underivable here-ness and thus-ness, as I affirm my own existence and myself; to make no longer any difference between the I and the Thou; to regard the Thou entirely as a part of my life, no longer to make a severance between the spirit of the Thou and my own spirit, but to draw the Thou entirely within my own territory and, as it were, to make the I and the Thou one—that is love. Where this is done, there the greatest miracle, the true miracle, happens.

2. Two Kinds of Love

Because the whole significance of this is so seldom understood, we must clarify it somewhat further by distinguishing it from some other qualities which have a similar appearance. Every collective experience has an apparent kinship with such fellowship; for example, in the case of the nation which is conscious of itself as a nation, and where one man feels himself bound to another as his fellow national, an experience that is shared in war or in great hours of the nation's history. Here we often speak of love and fellowship. But in truth what we have here is something quite different. What we have to do with here is not a relation of confrontation between I and Thou, in which the I, as it were, opens his heart to the Thou. What we have to do with here is the expansion of the individual self to a collective self. I do not say that this is something worthless, or something that ought not to be. I only say that it is not love in the biblical sense of the word. The love of one's nation is a collective egoism, which at once discloses its nature as such by the way in which we meet people who do not belong to this collective. Collective units are just as egoistic and exclusive in relation to other collectives as any egoistic individual can be.

To enlarge a self to a collective is by no means to make it a loving self, and to fuse a self with another into a collective is by no means to acknowledge it as a Thou. Here there is a unity of fusion, but no real fellowship.

The same thing is even more evidently true where the I and the Thou band together to achieve a common goal. Community of interest is not true fellowship. For we are not really concerned with the other man, but each of us uses the other man to achieve a determinate purpose. Whether this is something of purely external use—for example, a material good, as

in the case of a society pursuing a business interest, or whether we have to do with an aesthetic or other cultural and mental aim such as that of a literary society or a philosophical club or the like—makes no difference. In every case we have to deal with an association which is concerned, not with persons as such, but with an intellectual pursuit which people follow.

Somewhere in the middle between these two types there stands what is described in certain languages, at least in German, by the same word as the love of the New Testament, although we have here something entirely different, namely, *eros* in the widest sense of the word. Where one human being takes pleasure in another, whether it be in the narrower erotic sense or in the wider sense—pleasure in his body, his mind, his way of life, his character, or the like—a bond comes into being which seems very closely akin to what the New Testament calls love, but is really as far removed from it as the earth from the sky. For, as Plato so profoundly realized, this *eros* is always a relationship of fulfillment: it is a bond that comes into being between *ploutes* and *penia,* between overflow and lack; it is a desire in the higher and more refined sense of the word, but it is and remains a desire. We seek and value each other because of what one has to offer the other, physically, mentally, psychologically, or in some other way. The desire is awakened by a delight, and satisfies itself in a pleasure in one another. Whether this satisfaction is physical or spiritual is a matter of indifference. The difference between heavenly and earthly love is not that the one is sensuous and the other spiritual, but this: that the one, whether spiritual or sensuous, is not directed to the person himself but to something *in* the person, something that I desire, something that enriches and delights me, while love in the New Testament sense does not desire and does not enjoy, but is simply there for the other person.

This meaning of love was first clearly shown to the world through Jesus Christ. But, as Luther emphasizes, men have somehow always known, even though not with full clarity, that the relationship between men should be of this kind. It is not in this—that Jesus Christ made clear the meaning of love to men

—that his true revelation consists; Jesus is not a lawgiver who tells men what they ought to be. The command, "Thou shalt love thy neighbor as thyself," is—to quote Luther again—written in the hearts of men; the whole law, and therefore this its quintessence, is known to man from the creation. And yet we can say, with just as much justice though in another sense, "What love is, man can only know when he knows God's love in Jesus Christ." This remarkable twofold truth can only be understood by us if we now turn to the general question, "What is the basis of this love?" We all know without any doubt—whether we acknowledge it in theory and follow it in practice is not for the moment in question—we know from our conscience that we should love our neighbor as ourselves. This is what the law tells us in our hearts. But our knowing it does not guarantee our doing it. Indeed, it does not even guarantee the acknowledgment that we ought to do it. Our conscious will is something different from the law in our conscience, and the law in our conscience is something different from what we actually do. But whence comes this law in our conscience, and whence the gulf, and whence comes the bridge that spans the gulf—if indeed there is such a thing?

3. Of the New Man

We have already answered the first two questions in the earlier sections. Because man is created in God's Word, the law of love is inscribed in his heart. For love is the content of the Word of God. But the fact that this love is known to us only as law, as the "Thou shalt" and not as an accepted reality, is the same thing as this, that the cleft is in *us*. That we know of love only as law comes from the fact that we have fallen through self-will, through sin, away from the divine love as our life. Sin has the double effect that God's will becomes to us mere law, a "Thou shalt" challenge, and that the cleft between "ought" and "will," between "ought" and "is," arises in us. Instead of being a personal and living thing, responsibility has become abstract and legalistic. Therefore, although we have the law of love in us, we cannot rightly know what love is. For love is just precisely what withdraws itself from all legalistic laying down of norms. The legalistic command to love conceals from us the very meaning of love. So long as we know of love only as something demanded of us, we do not rightly know what it is. We know, and yet we do not know. And that is the state of affairs with men's knowledge, apart from the revelation in Christ.

But in Jesus Christ, as we said, it happens that the Word of the origin, which is something quite different from the word of the law, and yet is what the law really intends, comes again to us. Love, not as something demanded of us but as something bestowed upon us, not as law but as gift, as grace, as God's love, which bestows itself on the man who opposes it, which as forgiving love leads us back to the origin, and as redeeming love brings the consummation into view—this is the content of the New Testament proclamation, the proclamation of Christ.

But this proclamation is only different from something that we already know because it is a report of a real happening. If the gospel gave us a mere idea of love it would be nothing new, for we all of us have the idea of love within us, at least in principle. What we lack is not the idea but the reality. In Jesus Christ love comes to us as God's reality, love as our original life from God, as that Word, light, and life of the beginning which became flesh, which encounters us as historical human reality. It is of this happening of love, of this fact of history, that the gospel—the glad message—tells us.

I said that for this reason it is only here that we know even the meaning of love as distinct from justice or from *eros*, from a fellowship of interest or from collective self-love. In contrast to all this, the meaning of love is here disclosed as sacrifice, as self-bestowing love that desires nothing but simply communicates itself. "The Son of man came not to be ministered unto, but to minister, and to give his life a ransom for many." At this point, where the meaning of the divine love is revealed to us, the meaning also of true human love is revealed. And note this: these are not two things, but one and the same. The divine love, which is here in action, is itself true human love.

This means that love is not a human possibility but the divine possibility. But this is not to be understood as if it could not enter into human existence, but on the contrary in the sense that it is only through love that human existence is established as genuinely human. The life of man only receives true humanity in the moment that its life-principle is no longer within itself, but is in the divine love. Thus, as we first acknowledged, man has his true life in the Word of God, in the love of God. When the Word of God, the love of God in Jesus Christ, is bestowed again upon man, at the very same moment that he receives in faith God's Word of love, love is bestowed upon him. "Therefore being justified by faith, we have peace with God . . . and the love of God is shed abroad in our hearts by the Holy Spirit." When it happens that man allows God's Word of love to be spoken to him—this love which embraces the fallen one and unites him again with itself, which does away with the separation that the sin of man had created—the original vital connection, the original life in the love of God, is restored.

Certainly it is necessary here to repeat what was already said above: that this new life still has the old alongside it. Not on the same level, but as something fundamentally invalidated and put out of action. But so long as this earthly mode of existence continues, it also continues to be true that the old life once and again troubles the new, just as the weeds which have been cleared away, repeatedly grow afresh. Life in the love of God is, as it were, deposited like a new stratum over the old, over the life centered in me myself. But from the former mode of life, thus concealed, there repeatedly thrust upward into the new mode, manifestations of life—or, rather, manifestations of death. The victory of the new status of life is thus not unchallenged, but is violently called in question. But in principle it is established, and in principle the old is no longer taken into account. "If any man be in Christ, he is a new creature; the former things are done away, behold, all things are become new." But the new thing is life in love—in the love of God which is now "shed abroad in our hearts by the Holy Spirit."

4. Of Preaching

This will have to be made good in connection with the problem of fellowship. Up to this point we have always spoken of faith only as an event in the individual life, while we spoke of sin as a communal life or else as a solidary condemnation to death. We saw earlier that the whole of humanity is one *body of death* through sin. We have tried to understand the old formulations of the fall—inherited sin, the sin of humanity— in their true biblical sense. But now the knowledge of love as the new life-principle must vindicate itself by showing that in contrast with the body of death in which the individual is a member through his sin, there exists a *body of life,* in which every man participates through faith. The New Testament—and Christian experience—in fact speaks of such a body. It calls it, more precisely, not merely a body of life—for "life" is too indefinite a concept—it names it rather after the life-principle itself that establishes and communicates this life, after Jesus Christ, and speaks therefore of the Body of Christ as the new life-context in which the individual stands through faith.

Another expression for this same fact is the *ekklesia.* This word is hard to translate. Luther complained that the word "church," by which we are accustomed to render it, is a blind and unintelligible and even misleading word, because in this context we at once think of particular institutions, legal structures, and the like, which do indeed have something to do with that Church which is the Body of Christ, but which are not simply to be equated with this Body. The Body of Christ is primarily simply the particular life context or context of persons in which, through faith, a man stands with Christ, and, through him, with others who have the same faith.

Through Jesus Christ, through that Word of the beginning which is the Word of love, the individual man is released from the isolation of his solitary self, from his self-imprisonment and self-ingrownness, and joined to the divine Thou. Faith creates fellowship with God through fellowship with Christ, or in fellowship with Christ. The human self is once again in its true place, namely, in God. Only there can it rightly exist, in this bond and conjunction. The I has once again the divine Thou as the foundation of its life. The I breathes again in this air in which alone it can live, and this breathing we call prayer in the name of Jesus Christ. Prayer as answer to the divine Word is the first, the primary, expression of life of the new-created man. But we cannot just remain at this point. From the outset we have kept our eye on the individual, and made an abstraction from which we must now again depart. The Word of Christ does not encounter the individual in a vacuum, coming down direct from heaven. This Word encounters him in its proclamation through men. Just as Jesus Christ became man, and entered into a historical mode of existence, so must also the Word about him come to us in historical fashion—that is, through men. This happens through every kind of human witness to Jesus Christ—through preaching, through instruction, through simple witness from man to man, through pastoral care. But this witness is itself not independent, nor merely spontaneously generated. It is made by authority of Jesus Christ himself. Everyone who has received the Word and so has become a disciple must pass on what he has received, and become a witness. That this proclamation be made in orderly fashion, proclamation is also committed as preaching, a discipline with special rules of its own, to particular persons who are specially fitted for it. This is a very far-reaching theme, which cannot be dealt with here. In a moment we shall speak of a special form of this Word, the so-called sacraments.

But first of all this point must be made clear. Nobody comes in touch with Jesus Christ without coming in touch with men. Jesus Christ gives his Word only through men. Even the Bible was written by men, translated by men; it is printed and sold by men. And these will be the same men who interest themselves in the propagation of the Bible and know themselves responsible for its proclamation by the spoken word. This attachment of the Word to men is not an accident; this is what ought to be. For the same man who is separated from God by sin is cut off also from men by the same sin. He is without fellowship. We saw indeed that sin and lack of fellowship are one and the same thing. Lack of fellowship with God works itself out as lack of fellowship with men. When man is drawn out of his lack of fellowship with God, he is at the same time drawn out of his isolation in relation to men. He receives the Word of Christ from men, and by its means he is made dependent on men, and bound to them.

5. *The "Visible" Word, the Sacraments*

Admittedly this is at first an external bond. But these men who proclaim God's Word to him, disclose themselves to him—I am speaking in New Testament terms—both as believers and as men who seek to enfold him, not only in God's love, but in their own. The same act of communication which is intended to create the bond with God is intended also to create the bond with men, and where the one thing happens the other must also happen. In order to make it quite clear to ourselves, let us think back to the first Christians. These first disciples proclaimed the message of Christ's redemption through all the world: they did it from the compunction of faith—in obedience to God's will; but they did it also from the compunction of love, because they reckoned the men who were separated from them as of their number, knew themselves bound to them in solidary manner both in sin and in the divine redemption. "For God so loved the world that he gave his Son, that whosoever believeth in him should not perish, but have everlasting life." Everyone to whom they proclaimed the Word was to them a man beloved by Christ, and thus a man to be loved in Christ's name. The command to proclaim the Word to all was at the same time the command to enfold all in this love of Christ. And where a man opened his heart, where a man believed, then at that moment he was united not only to Christ but to these people of Christ's. There he became a member of the fellowship of Christ, the *ekklesia*, the Body of Christ.

This became quite specially clear in one form of the divine Word of which we have not yet spoken, in the so-called sacraments. I say "so-called" because this concept is really not a biblical but a heathen one. We prefer to speak of baptism and the Lord's Supper. Through baptism a man was incorporated in Christ's Body, taken up into the fellowship of believers, which as such was at the same time a fellowship of the loving brethren. And this happened by his becoming a participant in the sacrifice of Jesus Christ, through his also surrendering himself as a sacrifice to Christ. The once-for-allness of baptism was in a special manner the sign of the once-for-allness of the sacrifice of Christ, and the irrevocability of the decision for Christ. The man who was baptized had thereby surrendered his right to himself, and was henceforth one who belonged to Christ, a member of his Body, and thereby a fellow member with all other members. The Body of Christ is the fellowship of those who belong to Christ.

And so was it also with the second sign, the Lord's Supper or Last Supper. Here it was a case not of being received into the community but of being maintained in it. The Lord's Supper is therefore not a once-for-all event, but one that is continually repeated. It gives the clearest expression to the fact that the fellowship with Christ is a fellowship involving the whole of life, a participation of the whole man in the whole Christ, but at the same time a real fellowship of life with all fellow believers. The Lord's Supper bound in visible fashion all believers into a real unity, a solidary whole. Nowhere does the Body of Christ become so clearly visible as in the Lord's Supper. The Christian community is therefore above all a eucharistic community. Here, too, there was a participation in the sacrifice of Christ, which brings reconciliation and redemption, which signs and seals the real bond of union, the incorporation into the divine love. But in this case it is the constantly repeated, ever-renewed life—the ever-renewed pulsebeats which come from the heart and supply the whole body with the blood—that makes the body a living whole.

But this fellowship at the Lord's Supper was at the same time a life-fellowship, in the sense that it was just here, in the *agape*, in the love-feast, that the one gave to the other from what he himself possessed, and that those who were united with one another in the love-feast knew each other once more as brothers who were bound to one another in life and in death, who above all else owed one another mutual brotherly help in all things, or, rather, did not merely owe it but gave it willingly. For the love of God was shed abroad in their hearts through the Holy Ghost, and was shed abroad anew, through the Holy Supper. The fellowship of the Lord's Supper was not—and must not be—separated from the practical daily fellowship in life, in which one brother helps another in bodily and spiritual things.

The Apostle Paul spoke with sufficient clarity about this Body of Christ as a fellowship in love. There is no possible doubt that this—if I may so call it—fellowship in divine service or cult was at the same time a fellowship in the service of man, a moral or practical fellowship. For Paul did not recognize any other faith than one that "proves itself effectual in love." If faith is simply inclusion within the love of God, the obtaining of a share in the power of the divine love, yet this faith must also *vindicate* this character by showing itself as a power to love. For as in all great and holy things, so in the case of this greatest and holiest, there are surrogates which look like the real thing, a cheap sham faith which can be mistaken for faith so long as we do not inquire into it too closely, and which has just as little to do with real faith as gold tinsel has with real gold. The gold must stand the assayer's test. The test of true faith is love. There is a "faith" which does not stand this test. It is then not a real living fellowship with the living God and the living Christ, but a mere theoretical conviction, a mere faith of the head, a theological idea, intellectual assent to the doctrine of the Church. This faith, the Bible teaches, as do the Reformers, is useless. This reminds us of the thesis that we laid down earlier. Faith is a relation of persons, not of ideas. Faith is the real apprehension of my person by the real person of Jesus Christ. In this relationship words are only a means, for the true Word is Jesus Christ himself. The word in the grammatical sense is a necessary means; without this word in the grammatical sense, the connection cannot be made. But the fact remains that the word is only a means, because the true Word is Jesus Christ, the true Word of the beginning in whom we were created.

Just for this reason it is important that in addition to proclamation of the Word in the grammatical sense—that is, in addition to preaching, instruction, witness, and the like—we have also this other form of the Word, the visible happening in baptism and the Lord's Supper, where something visible is done to us, in order that we should take note of the fact that God's Word is an acting reality. It is particularly in its character as a fellowship of love, as brotherhood, as a life shared together, that the Church requires these "sacraments." The sacraments have a mysterious but undeniable relationship to fellowship as such. There, if anywhere, Christians have experienced down the ages that where two or three are gathered together in the name of Christ, there he is in the midst of them.

The figure of the Body is especially used by Paul to clarify a special problem, namely, the problem of individuality and fellowship. We see humanity in its history constantly swinging in one direction or the other between these two poles: collectivism and individualism. Individualism, the self-assertion of the individual as individual, destroys fellowship; we have had abundant experience of this in the last century, in the economic as well as the political individualism of the classical era of liberalism. Through the principle of the autonomy of reason, modern man has received an essentially individualist stamp, for the autonomous reason makes every man independent of his neighbor, sets a man on his own, and thus isolates him from his neighbor. But now we see how the flight back to nature from this individualism, the collectivism of the urges of blood and instinct, simply swings back to the opposite extreme. The rights of the individual are violently suppressed, the individual in his particularity is trodden down, everything is leveled off, and life falls a victim to a dismal stereotyped routine, an order of compulsory uniformity and regulation, which have just as little relationship to fellowship as the former anarchy. Today the pendulum of human history is swinging again strongly to this side. On the right and on the left we see forms of social engineering which create the mass-man, and threaten to destroy all individual life. They are indeed understandable as reactions to the individualistic disintegration, but they will just as inevitably beget again the individualistic reaction.

6. The Church

Only the reality of the *corpus Christi* can solve this dilemma for us. The first thing to say about every man is that as an individual he has his being in Jesus Christ, in the Word of God. Everyone is created and called as an individual by God, everyone must answer to him as an individual, everyone must die as an individual and pass through the divine judgment. The responsibility in faith is that of the individual, and the love which comes from faith is love for the individual. We can say: What the individual as an individual is, the personal responsibility of the individual, the Word of God alone shows us. "Here stand I, I can do no other, so help me God. Amen." It is to me, the individual, that God speaks his Word. There is no Christian faith of the masses—so far as there is such a thing, it is a surrogate; faith is the loneliest of all experiences. God's eye looks at you, this individual, out of eternity, and when you see it, you become a believer. No second person can become a witness of this happening. It happens in the deepest, eternal solitude.

But when this happens you are no longer an isolated individual; not only because God is now your ever-present Thou, but because you are in this same moment given your place in the Body of Christ, in the fellowship, in the *ekklesia*. One cannot get God as Father without at once getting men as one's brothers, some of them as brothers who know themselves as sons of God and my brothers, the true Body of Christ; and the others as men whom it is our task to make members and brothers. Through faith the individual is brought into the all-embracing fellowship, so that all divisions disappear. Here the deepest separation, that between the sexes, disappears—"here there is neither male nor female." Here the separation between the races disappears— "Here there is neither Jew nor Greek"; that between levels of culture—"Here there is neither Scythian nor barbarian"; that between poor and rich, for here there is no longer property, but only stewardship for God and service to the brethren.

But although these differences are in principle abolished, individual particularity is not stamped down or ironed out. But as a body has many different members, so the Church of Christ has need of many kinds of gifts and services. It is only within the new context, which makes all equal, that the differences between individuals come to their true fruition. They no longer divide; on the contrary, it is only by them that we are truly bound together. Through the different gifts and needs of each, one can serve another and be served by him; life is lived as bestowal and the receiving of help. Where love rules, the problem of individuality and collectivity is solved. Each is this particular individual, and is allowed to be so, but his individuality is not self-centered or self-originated, but has its origin in God and exists for the sake of others. His particularity becomes an endowment for special service, a *charisma*. Within the spiritual unity of the Body of Christ there are many *charismata*, and each fits its owner for a special service, and makes it his duty.

To these spiritual gifts correspond exactly the *diakoniai,* the services rendered. The fine word *noblesse oblige* here receives a new meaning: every endowment signifies at the same time a special duty to serve.

7. *The Resolution of a Spiritual Dilemma*

Just as the problem of individual and collective is solved here, so is it with the problem of the concrete and the universal. Each is united with each, but not in the sense of a general enthusiasm for humanity—"Be embraced, ye millions!"—but in the sense of the most concrete practical activity: love of our neighbor. Love is quite concrete; it does not exhaust itself in humanitarian feelings, but it *does* for our *neighbor* what he needs. But this obligation and readiness to serve knows no limits. This neighbor can indeed be the Samaritan who is "no concern of mine," the man who is separated from me by the barrier of race, of religion, of party, of class. In range of possibility the Christian spirit of brotherhood is absolutely universal; in reality it is always quite concrete and special. And while everyone is enjoined to do what lies nearest to his hand, he is at the same time challenged to bestir himself as one who is responsible with others for the extension of the kingdom of God in the whole world, who shares in the work, who is ready to go anywhere for his Master, who shares in the joy and the sorrow, the pride and the shame, of all that concerns the Body of Christ throughout the world. "For where one member suffers, all the members suffer with it; and where one is honored, all rejoice with it."

This is the impression we get of the primitive Christian community, as we see it, for example, in the letters of the Apostle Paul. What concreteness of neighborly love, what a universal horizon and interest! The smallest duty lying to hand is to be taken with utter seriousness, as the practical task immediately enjoined; and at the same time the vision of the whole that embraces heaven and earth, the coming kingdom of God, is not for a moment to be lost from sight. "World citizens" was the title that the old Stoics proudly gave themselves. To be citizens of heaven—that is the calling which Paul opposes to this as the calling of the Christian. But this heavenly citizenship of faith and hope does not estrange them from tasks of daily practical reality. Rather does it incite them with full seriousness to engage in these tasks, from the motive of neighborly love. The most universal thing that exists is the Christian hope; everything in heaven and earth is here bound up in one vital unity, in the kingdom of God; and the most concrete thing that exists is Christian love, which takes absolutely in earnest the individual in his unique particularity of the here and now and thus. *This* is the fellowship of the *ekklesia*, so far as it is really "in Christ."

8. *The Body of Christ*

I have spoken of the Church of the New Testament. And thus of something that belongs to the past? I could not have done it if it only belonged to the past. We can speak of Jesus Christ and his fellowship only because and insofar as he himself and it itself are a contemporary reality. But the gulf between what is today called Church or Christianity and what we see before us in the New Testament as the fellowship of Christ is certainly a big one. A tremendous amount of the substitute for faith of which we spoke has mixed itself with what is authentic, real faith, and the consequence of this is that there is much Christianity—sham Christianity—which shows its inauthenticity by the lack of witness through practical acts of commitment in love. This is the chief reason why the reputation of Christianity in the world has sunk so low. The obstacle is not the dogmas, but the lovelessness of Christians. Admittedly, the message of the cross remains the greatest stone of stumbling, because it represents the frontal attack on our autonomous humanity. The message of the cross bows us, breaks us, in order to form us anew as men of God, as the men that he created us. But if this astounding message is so often not heard, or is ignored or despised today, this offense that lies in the nature of the thing itself is not the only cause, but the incredibility of the people who bear witness to it. It is still always so that where there is real Christian life, and where the Word is not contradicted by the life, there it always finds a multitude of eager hearers, and even today people crowd together to it, in order themselves to have the new and better thing that the others have. And here, too, it is evident that today as of old the Spirit of Jesus Christ solves problems of communal life that are otherwise insoluble.

Today, as never before in world history, mankind is in a strange situation. For the first time in world history, mankind is in the external sense one body, one closely knit fellowship sharing a common destiny. What happens in Tokyo is at once, even on the same day, not only known in London and Kapstadt, but is most sensitively felt, perhaps in the form of an economic or political panic. The farthest east and the farthest west are united to each other in a manner hitherto unknown. This has happened through the overcoming of spatial separation, through the unity of civilization, and through a certain external culture. And at the same time mankind is involved in perhaps never hitherto experienced disintegration, caused by the absence of every bond of spiritual fellowship, every acknowledged higher authority over all the peoples. For this reason this body of mankind is convulsed with almost unprecedented pains. Mankind is incapable of solving the resultant problem with its own resources. There *is* one solution, only one, but this is the solution in the absolute sense: the Body of Christ. It is the answer to the search for fellowship.

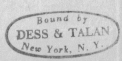